A Focus on Hope

Fifty Resilient Students Speak

Erik E. Morales
Frances K. Trotman

UNIVERSITY PRESS OF AMERICA,® INC.
Lanham • Boulder • New York • Toronto • Plymouth, UK

Copyright © 2011 by
University Press of America,® Inc.
4501 Forbes Boulevard
Suite 200
Lanham, Maryland 20706
UPA Acquisitions Department (301) 459-3366

Estover Road
Plymouth PL6 7PY
United Kingdom

Library of Congress Control Number: 2010930634
ISBN: 978-0-7618-5271-1 (clothbound : alk. paper)
ISBN: 978-0-7618-5272-8 (paperback : alk. paper)
eISBN: 978-0-7618-5273-5

I dedicate this book to all of the resilient role models and inspirations I have been fortunate enough to have with me at critical points in my personal and professional life. Specifically, I would like to dedicate this text to my mother, Ms. Nina Morales; my father, Dr. Danilo Morales; my sister, Ms. Marisa Gonzalez; and my brother, Mr. Henning Morales. I would also like to thank my loving and supportive wife Tami, and my beautiful children, Keith and Cassie- Thank you for everything! Furthermore, I would like to send a special message of appreciation to the New Jersey City University Deborah Cannon Partridge Wolfe College of Education, and specifically to my colleagues in the Department of Elementary and Secondary Education. Finally, I would like to thank my students, virtually all of whom exhibit profound resilience on a daily basis and without complaint.

—*Erik E. Morales, PhD.*

I would like to dedicate this book to my beautiful, resilient grandchildren: Keith Durval and Cassidy Rose Morales, and Alyssa Marie and Amanda Michelle Perna. They already make the world a better place.

—*Frances K. Trotman, PhD.*

Contents

1	Introduction	1
2	Meeting the Students and Capturing Their Stories	9
3	The "Resilience Cycle": An Overview	16
4	The Cycle in Context: Spoke 1 "Recognizing Reality"	20
5	The Cycle in Context: Spoke 2 "Manifesting Help"	30
6	The Cycle in Context: Spoke 3 "Synthesizing Resources"	38
7	The Cycle in Context: Spoke 4 "Evaluating and Enhancing"	58
8	The Cycle in Context: Spoke 5 "Developed Habits and Goals"	63
9	Facilitating Resilience: Practical Implications	68

Appendix A: Resilient Students' Demographic Information   79

Appendix B: The Resilience Cycle   81

Appendix C: Resilient Students' Institutional Data   83

Appendix D: Resilient Students and Major Protective Factors   85

Appendix E: Major Psychological Stressors Associated with
    Academic Achievement   87

Appendix F: Individual Student Demographics (N=50)   89

References   91

Index   93

Chapter One

Introduction

WHAT IS ACADEMIC RESILIENCE?

Academic resilience refers to the process and outcome of students who, despite coming from statistically "at-risk" backgrounds, *do* succeed academically. The academically resilient are essentially "the statistical elite." They are the ones who succeed where educational achievement gap data insist they *should* fail. As framed in this text, they are born and raised facing the infamous and ubiquitous stressors of ethnic minority and low socio-economic status (i.e. violence, sub-par public schools, rampant drug abuse, institutional racism, etc.). However, despite exposure to this myriad of social malady, they manage to ascend through the educational system and excel academically.

Basically, resilient students are anomalies, in many ways paralleling Du-Bois' (1903) "talented tenth" of exceptional and high achievers. And while they are unique in the sense of their extraordinary achievement, that in other ways they are very much the same as their lower achieving peers. Because they can be so similar in core ways, the basic question of why and how their results are so different serves as an enduring question for this and virtually all resilience research. This question leads to the academic resilience concept and resilience theory.

Understanding and applying resilience theory requires a more drastic paradigm shift than most people initially recognize. At its core, resilience theory necessitates a belief that virtually all young people have an innate and natural resilience *capacity* that makes positive, healthy development a natural outgrowth of their existence and humanity. This is why the term "resilient" is so appropriate, resilience means bouncing *back*, as in reverting back to an

original state. Ideally, the original state is one of health and positive development. Thus, resilience theory operates under the premise that all are innately
able to succeed as long as environmental stress factors are mitigated.

It should be pointed out that there are different types of resilience identified in the resilience literature. Originally, psycho-social resilience was the
most common type studied (see Garmenzy, 1991; Rutter, 1979; and Werner
& Smith, 1992 for seminal works). This involved samples of individuals who
had been exposed to psychological stressors (e.g. poverty, alcoholic or schizo-
phrenic parents, etc.) who then grew into "well adjusted" adults. Therefore,
resilience in general necessarily focused on some form of psychosocial accomplishment whereas with *academic* resilience, *educational* achievement is
the logical and implicit end result.

The change in emphasis engendered by the resilience model, from failure
to success, mirrors to a certain extent model shifts in healthcare and psychology. Until recently, it was relatively rare to hear terms like "wellness" and
"preventative health" in the medical lexicon. However, more and more medical researchers are studying health in order to promote it. And while we are
not directly applying a medical model to education, (nor do we equate low
school performance with illness), there is a certain parallel in how medical
and educational issues are being addressed. This model shift has manifested
itself in the mental health field as well. The current zeitgeist in popular
psychology revolves around "happiness studies" and ways to increase happiness levels. This is more evidence for a changing focus, moving away from
problem-based approaches to individual and social issues (i.e. deficit models)
and toward a health orientation.

RESILIENCE RESISTANCE:
WHY THE OPPOSITION TO A RESILIENCE FOCUS?

The resilience shift is so drastic because in reality, most of our societal con-
structs are based on anti-resilient/negative thinking. Often times we operate
under the assumption that the well adjusted, inquisitive, success-oriented
individual is the exception rather than the rule. For example, in high schools
and universities, honors track and advanced placement programs are designed
for the numerical minority. The underlying assumption and message sent is
that only a relatively small percentage of the whole will be expected and able
to operate at such a level. Resilience theory on the other hand begins with
the assumption that innately all students will operate at such a level, and that
the reason they may not be currently is that too many environmental stressors
have forced them "off-track." As a result, resilience research seeks to under-

stand how students have overcome, evaded, or mitigated the stressors, in an attempt to apply what is learned to others.

Because we live in a nation—if not a world, but definitely a nation—that is disproportionately focused on the negative and the problematic, a focus on hope often engenders scorn, ridicule, pessimism, and skepticism. Contributing to this general cloud of negativity, we find four specific beliefs that, while erroneous, make people reticent to embrace optimism and resilience when it comes to schooling. These specious beliefs are stated below and then explored in greater detail:

1. By focusing on success, failure is neglected.
2. Documenting successful students and what they have done to be successful in essence blames those who have not been successful for their lack of success.
3. By profiling students who have been successful within the educational system, there is a tacit blessing of the efficacy of that system, as well as a dismissal of any injustice and unfairness inherent to it.
4. Because academic success for ethnically marginal students has often been correlated to assimilation, emphasizing academic success is, at times, akin to promoting communal/cultural/racial betrayal.

While on the surface these issues appear to have merit, ultimately they are hollow and potentially destructive belief systems resulting from fear and/or misunderstanding.

DEBUNKING MYTHS OPPOSING RESILIENCE STUDIES

Myth #1: By focusing on success, failure is neglected.

A focus on success inevitably *includes* an exploration of failure, but not from the "failure as a foregone conclusion" perspective. By utilizing resilience theory with success at the center, failure is then viewed how it should be—as an anomalous, unnatural, and unexpected outcome. If we truly expect no child to be left behind, then failure must move from the central focus of our expectation to the outskirts. When educators talk about raising standards and expectations it behooves all stake holders to address failure, not as an expectation, but rather as a consequence of improper or insufficient support.

Myth #2: Documenting successful students and what they have done to be successful, in essence blames those who have not been successful for their lack of success.

A resilience focus, as defined earlier, does not blame those who fail. On the contrary, it works on the assumption that their failures are unnatural outcomes, and that their true essence is to succeed. As a result the failure is framed as a consequence of environmental stressors that have served to undermine their resilience. A major benefit of this approach is that it never gets too late or the situation too dire. Ultimately, this is an empowering approach because the student retains his or his resilience capacity despite where he or she is, and what may have happened. To the contrary, deficit models not only focus overwhelmingly on failure, but also disempower the individual by placing virtually all influence/power in the environment, leaving him or her helpless. This is perhaps the most egregious crime that can be committed by well-meaning but misguided educators who operate under the determinist belief that the educational structure is so corrupt and so unjust that students are essentially impotent statistics being swept along by whatever currents or winds may come their way.

Myth 3: By profiling students who have been successful within the educational system, there is a tacit blessing of the efficacy of that system, as well as a dismissal of any injustice and unfairness inherent to it.

A resilience focus acknowledges the disparity of educational quality and opportunity between and among low and high socioeconomic, as well as between majority and minority students. Furthermore, as with our own research, most of the prescriptions to increase and spread resilience include substantive and structural improvements in the educational resources available to students. However, resilience research also acknowledges that as dysfunctional as some of these educational systems may be, there are still those who have managed to excel within them. As a result, the "achievement gap war" can be fought simultaneously on two fronts: One is to demand more and better educational resources, and the other is to help students manage whatever resources are available. The two are not mutually exclusive.

Myth 4: Because academic success for marginal students has often been correlated to assimilation, emphasizing academic success is at times akin to promoting community/cultural/ethnic betrayal.

The assimilation issue is among the most controversial and delicate when discussing the residence and achievement experiences of ethnic minorities. Individuals may or may not choose to assimilate; and may or may not assimilate to varying degrees. However, complete assimilation is not a prerequisite to academic resilience and achievement. While it is true that to a certain extent students from marginal backgrounds must adopt certain cultural practices (primarily speech/language patterns) in order to achieve academically, whether or not complete assimilation into the new culture is the result varies a great deal. There is "acculturation without assimilation" (Gibson, 1986) where students adopt certain behavioral characteristics of the mainstream culture in order to thrive in academia, but still retain essential aspects of their cultural backgrounds. Additionally, many students view their adaptation to academia in an additive manner, as opposed to a zero sum game. They don't view themselves as giving up an old culture and adopting a new one, rather they view themselves as becoming "more." Gandara (1995) and Gibson (1986) refer to this resilience phenomenon as "additive acculturation" and found it descriptive of many of the resilient students in their studies. Students like these view themselves as *expanding* who they are so that they can "fit in" to multiple academic and cultural groups.

Finally, for those who do choose to assimilate fully, they have the right to do so. Perhaps the biggest gift education provides is the ability to become someone else, someone new. If, as part of their academic resilience process, they embrace academia or middle class culture completely, then that is their choice and it should be honored. However, as far as the fifty students in this study, the vast majority remain close to their cultures and communities of origin, even as they excel in their academic pursuits.

Finally, perhaps the biggest obstacle to embracing a resilience perspective is one that is almost never articulated aloud but appears just below the surface, namely the belief that expecting all students to thrive is idealistic and Pollyanna. Because the idea is so incongruous with the current "education as competition" winners-and-losers model, it is easy to dismiss. However, those of us who are truly committed to excellence for all must begin with the premise that all people are born enthusiastic and curious learners, and though these nascent qualities may be dormant, they exist nonetheless.

KEY ELEMENTS OF RESILIENCE THEORY

Four elements often utilized in resilience theory are *risk factors, protective factors, vulnerability areas*, and *compensatory strategies* (Kitano & Lewis, 2005). *Risk factors* are (usually) environmental issues that place students in potential danger. These may include inferior schools, a culture of violence, or a lack of parental attention. All of these can place a student "a-risk." *Protective factors* are strengths students have (or can access) that work to mitigate the risk factors. These may include a caring relative, a strong work ethic, an internal locus of control, or a community organization (see Appendix D for a complete list of protective factors for students in this study and the percentage of them who identified each of the factors). A *vulnerability area* is a specific aspect of a student that manifests itself as problematic in a particular situation. For example, while a risk factor may be inferior schools resulting in a student's high school offering no math above geometry, a vulnerability area may be the student's low score on the math portion of the SAT. The risk factor becomes a vulnerable area in the context of the students' pursuits. *Compensatory strategies* are tactics that students use to overcome specific vulnerabilities or risk factors. For example, in the case above, the student may seek math tutoring or apply to a college that doesn't stress SAT scores in its admission policy. Those would be compensatory strategies.

While the resilience lexicon can get quite complex and nuanced, in this research we focus on broader categories of risk and protection. Simply put, risk factors are any issues that serve as obstacles to a student's growth and achievement. Protective factors include anything that mitigates the effects of existing risk factors and/or promotes growth, development, and achievement. Specific nuances and categories of risk and protective factors are explored in greater detail in further portions of this text. However, a significant "next step" which this text takes is to move beyond isolated factors and explore deeply the processes by which those factors are grouped and operate in order to produce the phenomenon known as "academic resilience."

WHY STUDY RESILIENCE?

The most important and obvious reason to study resilience is that knowing about something is an essential step toward being able to replicate and spread it. Instead of the majority of traditional educational research which has adopted a deficit approach, focusing on what is broken, resilience research asks the question *What does it look like when it works?* The importance of this shift in thinking cannot be underestimated. It sets up a perspective that promotes possibility and hope, two concepts that are in short supply when the educational prospects of minority and low socioeconomic youth are being discussed.

More thorough understandings of resilience can also bring us closer to two goals shared by most who are concerned with the promotion of academic achievement in America: The need for informed and effective approaches to educational initiatives, as well as an overall need to know more about the rapidly growing groups of ethnic minority students populating our schools and nation.

It is essential that initiatives and interventions designed to facilitate resilience are grounded in research and take into account the unique and often unobvious psych-social phenomena particular to students from backgrounds that have traditionally struggled academically. As Anderson (1998) warns, educators must not design academic enhancement initiatives for students of color that are based on Eurocentric research and norms (or perhaps even worse, no research at all). Research and American culture make obvious the fact that non-white Americans experience America in significantly different ways than the majority population. In order maximize the effectiveness of educational enhancement initiatives, educators must acknowledge and comprehend those differences, then employ what is learned.

The second primary reason to understand resilience is the ongoing goal of increasing general understanding of the experiences of the "other," and giving voice to those individuals. This unearthing of experience works to create intimacy across ethnicities, socioeconomic strata, and generations. In essence it helps to bridge gaping social chasms which remain despite current efforts.

MAJOR ASPECTS OF ACADEMIC RESILIENCE RESEARCH

Different forms and facets of academic resilience have been explored by various researchers. Key features to consider are degree of resilience, sub-populations, focus on protective factors, and the resilience process. These are all different angles and foci used to explore this complex phenomenon. Because resilience is by nature a lengthy process, a longitudinal approach of some kind must be employed. As a result, the most common qualitative instrument used in resilience research is the extended interview. During this process the resilient individual reflects on her or his academic history. The most common quantitative method is the use of follow up surveys, capturing the state of individuals at various points in their lives. Regardless of the methods used, an understanding of where one began, where one ended up, and what happened in between is the objective.

Degree of resilience is a relative term referring to the "distance traveled" by the resilient individual. That is, measuring where the students began and where they ended up. Looking at the extremes in seminal works, Gandara (1995) focused on poor Mexican Americans who ended up earning doctoral degrees in academic disciplines, law or medicine. On the more moderate end of the spectrum, Gale (1996) used a junior high school GPA minimum of 3.0/4.0. Our work lands somewhere in the middle: Ethnic minority/low SES status and a 3.0 GPA at the college level. Regardless of the parameters of the degrees of resilience, due to what we know about the historical and current correlation between ethnic minority status/low SES status and low academic achievement, any of the above can be termed academic resilience.

Another important attribute of resilience research is the increasing focus on sub-groups and the similarities and differences among them. Different resilient sub-groups explored include Mexican-Americans (Conchas, 2006; Gandara, 1995; Suarez-Orozco, 1995, Villanueva, 1996) African–Americans (Ford, 1996; Morales & Trotman, 2004; Winfield, 1991), Dominican-Americans (Morales, 2000), Puerto Ricans (Taylor & Wang, 2000) East-Asian immigrants (Gibson, 1986), Asian Americans (Crosnoe & Elder, 2004, Taylor & Wang, 2000) and Native Americans (McCubbin, Thompson, & Fromer, 1998). The two major benefits of focusing on sub-groups are context and exposure. By understanding how resilience occurs within specific sub-cultures, greater understanding of the nuances of specific processes is attained. Additionally, as discussed earlier, because academic research has historically tended to neglect minority groups, resilience research on neglected ethnic groups gives much needed voice to those groups.

Regardless of the specific samples, most resilience research is focused on the identification of key protective factors. This focus tends to isolate and decontextualize. As a result, much is known about what protective factors are prevalent in the lives of resilient individuals, but very little about the *process* by which these factors help produce resilience. Understanding process is essential from both a practical and theoretical standpoint. Understanding process allows for the creation of models and initiatives that are context specific. This context specificity allows for more effective interventions because those interventions take into account the psycho-social realities lived by the individuals. This is not to discount the importance of understanding protective factors, rather to recapitulate that understanding protective factors in isolation is an important first step in understanding the resilience process. As a result, in this text—specifically in the chapter on Spoke 3 (*Student Manages Her or His Protective Factors in Concert to Propel Her of Himself toward High Academic Achievement*)—there is an attempt to understand the components of resilience within the idiosyncratic contextual process of each individual life.

The observations and conclusions included in this text are based upon original research done on resilient men and women. Beginning in the late 1990's we have documented interviews with fifty academically resilient individuals from a variety of racial, ethnic, and socioeconomic backgrounds. In-depth qualitative studies of this type normally include samples of between three and seven students. A qualitative study of 50 students allows for an extraordinary level of breadth and depth.

Chapter Two

Meeting the Students and Capturing Their Stories

THE STUDENTS

The fifty young people who eventually became the "sample population" of this book shared several key background characteristics, but were also highly individualistic and representative of a range of institutional backgrounds and experiences (See Appendix C for details). One reason for this diversity is that the sample, and consequently the data, was gathered over a period of time beginning in 1997 and extending to 2004. As the researchers continued their work in the field, we continued to encounter students meeting the background criteria and added them to our pool.

As discussed earlier, when using academic resilience theory, there must be certain pre and post criteria met. The meeting of these pre (status where the student began) and post (what the student achieved) criteria define academic resilience as long as they correlate with established/statistical norms of "exceptional" academic achievement. Normally, resilience theory uses national statistical data to define what exceptional is. Basically, if the student's academic outcome is significantly higher than what most from his/her starting point would be expected to achieve, then resilience is present.

The shared background and achievement data for all of the fifty students were:

Pre criteria:
- Each student had parents with limited educational backgrounds (HS graduates or below) and who worked in low or semi-skilled jobs (Low SES), and each student self-identified as an ethnic minority.

Post Criteria:
- At the time of interview each student had completed a *minimum* of 30 college credits and had a minimum grade point average of 3.0 (using a 4-point scale).

The rationale for using these criteria are based on statistical evidence indicating that individuals meeting the pre-resilience criteria would be unlikely to meet the post-resilience criteria (American Council on Education, 2006). As a result, these students are by definition academically resilient.

ETHNIC/RACIAL BACKGROUND

While all of the students are U.S. citizens, there is a great deal of ethnic and racial diversity within the group. The students' race/ethnicities were determined solely based on the students' self-identification on prospective research participant application forms. This was done to respect the students' rights to claim their own identities in ways in which they are comfortable. As a result, there are various categories of identification used to describe the students (e.g. race, ethnicity, nationality, etc.).

All of the students grew up the northeastern part of the United States, primarily in New York City and Northern New Jersey. Some were born in other areas and/or moved around somewhat, but for the most part they were all reared in this part of the country.

By far, the largest groups of students (See appendix A for full demographic details) are African American (N=21) and Hispanic (N=20). All of the African American students were born in the northern United States and many had recent ancestors who migrated north from the south after the Civil War. They all identified English as their sole home language.

While the Hispanic students all identified themselves as such, the specific Spanish speaking countries from which they or their families hailed represents its own measure of diversity. Additionally, many of the students had mothers and fathers who came from different Spanish speaking countries; three had only one parent from a Spanish speaking country. Of the twenty, nine further identified themselves as Puerto Rican, seven as Dominican (from the Dominican Republic), two as Cuban, one as Mexican, and one as Ecuadorian. All but three of the Hispanic students identified themselves as bilingual and Spanish as their primary home language. Additionally, half of them (N=10) attended bilingual or ESL classes at some point in their educational careers.

Interestingly, a full 10% (N=5) of the students identified themselves as "Bi-racial, Black and White." Of this group, four had White mothers and Black fathers, and one a White father with a Black mother.

Four of the students self-identified as hyphenated Americans from non-Spanish speaking countries; two Haitian American, one Jamaican American, and one Guyanese American. Each of these students spoke the mother tongue of their parents' birth country at home.

While clearly this sample consists of a true cross-section of races, ethnicities and nationalities, significantly, all of these students viewed themselves as "minorities" and "people of color." Thus, in describing their experiences they often view their worlds in terms of "them" (White people) and "us" people of color. Consequently, while this group of students is indeed highly diverse, in some very important ways a shared sense of "otherness" existed which was highly significant to their educational journeys.

GENDER

Sixty-two percent of these resilient students were female, leaving thirty-eight percent male. This ratio is somewhat consistent with national data on the disparity of female versus male students throughout the country, especially when looking at students of color.

While gender significance is not a major focus of this text, in reviewing salient differences between the experiences of the female and male students several key differences arise. In reviewing the data, the following four *significant* and pronounced thematic differences arose when comparing female and male resilience experiences:

- Females faced more resistance to the pursuit of their college and career goals from family members and significant others as compared to males.
- Males relied on racial/ethnic obligation, identity and pride for motivation more than females.
- Females used their post college professional goals as motivation more than did males.
- When identifying influential mentors (both during high school and college) sharing the same gender of the potential mentor was significantly more important for the males than for the females.

How these thematic concepts actually contribute to the creation of protective factors and the overcoming of risk factors will be explored throughout the text.

PARENTAL HOUSEHOLD STATUS

Perhaps not surprisingly, only about half of the students (48%) grew up with both parents in the home. The remaining students spent the majority of their childhoods with only one parent. Significantly, *none* of the single parent households consisted of a father. Consequently, not only did a full fifty-two percent of the sample not grow up with their fathers in their households, but when looking at the males (for whom a father would presumably serve as more of a crucial role model) a disproportionate number 12/17 (70.5%) lacked fathers in the home. Evidence from the interviews indicates that for these students in particular, male mentors were especially valuable. This reality supports the point noted above that male students were significantly more likely to connect with male mentors as opposed to their female counterparts. The importance of academic male role models for the male study participants is explored throughout the text.

PARENTS' EDUCATION LEVEL

As identified in the pre and post criteria above, all of the students had parents who had not earned college degrees. As per Appendix A, most of the parents had high school completion as their highest level of education. A small minority of parents had not earned high school diplomas, and an even smaller percentage had attended some college. While many of the detailed consequences of the parents' under-education are explored throughout the text, a salient reality which grew from parents' educational and financial statuses was the lack of access to technology at home. Very few of the sample population had access to computers at home, and in their narratives the consequences of this reality became pronounced.

STUDENTS' HOME LOCALES

The vast majority (80%) of the sample population grew up in urban settings, primarily in the northeastern part of the United States. Many of these cities (or sections of the cities) had suffered "white flight" and are now virtually all African American, Hispanic, and immigrant. The stark realities of these environments, including higher crime rates, lower performing public schools, and increased exposure to gangs, drugs, and violence, profoundly contributed to the challenges and obstacles facing these students. This impact was evident not only in theory and statistics, but in the reality of the student narratives as well.

Sixteen percent (N=8) of the students grew up in working class suburban areas and four percent (N=2) in areas that could be described as rural. However, these 10 students did move around and spend some time in urban areas as well. While these specific students may not have been exposed to the intensity of risk factors of their urban peers, they still had to overcome socioeconomic disparities in comparison with their wealthier peers.

At the time of the interviews the participants were between the ages of 18 and 26, with most of them being 19 or 20. The interview process was designed to capture students' memories of relatively recent academic experiences which lie at the heart of their resilience. For this reason, the participants' active involvement in their ongoing academic resilience at the time of the interviews was both strategic and intentional.

PARTICIPANT SELECTION

Of the fifty total participants, twenty-two were referred by college faculty and staff, seventeen responded to flyers posted around college campuses, and eleven were referred by friends of participants. Each was asked to provide college transcripts to document academic standing, while parental socioeconomic status (SES) and participants' racial identity were determined based on participant response alone.

QUALITATIVE AND QUANTITATIVE METHOD

An overriding purpose of this research initiative was to provide a *thorough* and *comprehensive* view of resilient individuals and *processes* of resilience. Because of this stated goal, and the fact that the academic resilience phenomenon is inherently complex, idiosyncratic, multidimensional, and understudied, primarily qualitative methodologies were employed.

A core belief of ours is that in order to understand an individual, one must understand how that individual views her or his world. With this emphasis, we have relied a great deal on both symbolic interactionism and phenomenology in doing our research. Broadly defined, phenomenology emphasizes the subjectivity of experience (Bogdan & Biklen, 1982; Geertz, 1973) and symbolic interactionism asserts that individuals create their own meaning from experience through their particular interaction with, and interpretation of, that experience (Blumer, 1969).

IN-DEPTH INTERVIEWING

Because we were so intent on understanding the individuals' worlds from their perspectives, we used the in-depth interview extensively. The in-depth interview is particularly effective for this purpose (Geertz, 1973; McCracken, 1998; Spradley, 1979; Rubin & Rubin, 1995; Watson & Watson-Franke, 1985). As McCraken (1988) writes "(the long interview) takes us into the mental world of the individual, to glimpse the categories or logic by which he or she sees the world" (p.9). Specific to resiliency, Liddle (1994) writes "The resiliency concept, although sounding abstract can be found in the narrative of the subjects interviewed. These respondents, with their powerful life stories, are indispensable to the evolution of the resiliency notion" (p. 170).

Specific to our study, each of the fifty students was interviewed a minimum of three times over the course of approximately six weeks. Each interview was audio-taped and transcribed at a later date. Following Kirk & Miller's (1986) inverted triangle—moving from the general to the specific—the initial interview gleaned background information, and the follow-up interviews explored and documented findings in detail. Finally, after the third interview, member-checks were conducted to address any extant contradictions, and to further establish the veracity of the researchers' findings. About 25% of the students (those who were working at the time) were compensated $10/hour for their time during the interviews.

DATA ANALYSIS

Consistent with the work of Lincoln & Guba (1985) and Rubin & Rubin (1995) throughout this research process, data collection and analysis were separate processes that were closely intertwined. Once initial data were gathered on each participant, analysis was done to identify *significant* protective and risk factors ("significant" in this study was operationalized as concepts or challenges that the participants believed were *absolutely crucial* to their academic success). Once significant factors were identified, subsequent interview transcripts were combed to elicit their processes of operation, and the possible presence of multiple factors operating together.

All interviews were transcribed. These transcriptions became part of the field logs. Ely (1991) describes the log as a cohesive history of the investigation. Additional components of the log included field notes, personal reflections and descriptions. These writings were then used to write lengthier writings called analytic memos (Bogdan & Biklen, 1982). The analytic memos allowed us to begin synthesizing thoughts and observations.

Consistent with Bogdan & Biklen (1982) the bulk of the actual data analysis process involved creating coding categories and concepts, and identifying emerging themes. The major categories which arose from this data analysis became the basis for the upcoming chapters identifying resilience components and processes.

This research process was continually engaged until both completeness and data saturation were achieved. Completeness is the principle of adding interviews until one is satisfied with the level of understanding for the given phenomenon (Rubin & Rubin, 1995). The saturation point is defined as the place in time when additional interviews add little to what has already been learned (Glaser & Strauss, 1965).

TRUSTWORTHINESS

As with virtually all social science research, the goal here was to capture and describe the "truth" about the relevant experiences of the research participants. In our case, we wanted to know exactly how these students were able to excel academically, with the goal of using that information to eventually form truths that may help others achieve similar levels.

To ensure as much as reasonably possible that we were being accurate in reporting our findings, we relied primarily on member checking (described earlier), triangulation, and external audits. Triangulation involves securing multiple sources of corroboration for a particular point. For example, if a student described a teacher as particularly important, we would identify multiple instances and situations where that student had described that teacher's efforts; the more instances, the more certain we are of that teacher's impact.

Chapter Three

The "Resilience Cycle": An Overview

The "Resilience Cycle" (See appendix B for Cycle graphic) is an original theoretical framework that captures major sequential steps in of the process of exceptional academic achievement of statistically at-risk students (aka *academic resilience*). Having evolved from original resilience research conducted by one of the authors during his doctoral dissertation, the framework has evolved as more studies have been conducted, and has been highlighted in a variety of subsequent research publications (Morales, 2000; Morales, 2008).

The Resilience Cycle addresses three major deficits of current resilience theory. First, a major focus of the Cycle is that it focuses on the resilience *process*, rather than simply identifying isolated variables. Identification of valuable protective factors is important, but in-depth understanding how these factors produce resilience is a next logical step which has received surprisingly little attention. It is for this reason that Chapter 6, which focused on the protective factor process, is significantly longer than the rest.

Second, unlike other approaches to resilience, the Cycle emphasizes and accounts for the idiosyncratic nature of resilience. Highly specific theories and frameworks are often not as valuable as they could be because they do not take into account core differences between and among students and their circumstances. The Resilience Cycle is general enough to incorporate these substantive differences, yet still cohesive enough to maintain commonalities.

Finally, an area which has received far too little attention in resilience theory is the enduring nature of resilience. Academic resilience requires *ongoing* achievement as students move into progressively more challenging and rigorous academic environments. Because the Resilience Cycle theory emphasizes how new and additional protective factors can become valuable as new challenges present themselves, it evolves along with the students' changing circumstances.

The Resilience Cycle includes a "hub" and the following five "spokes" (aka steps) representing the educational resilience process as demonstrated by the participants in this study. The theory is cyclical in that its progression tends to repeat itself as students enter new academic phases in their lives and face the accompanying challenges. Throughout the remainder of this text how each of the spokes was reflected in the students' narrative is presented in great detail. To introduce the reader to these central concepts, below are very brief descriptions of each step and the "hub."

SPOKE 1: THE STUDENT REALISTICALLY RECOGNIZES HER OR HIS MAJOR RISK FACTORS.

This first step captures the value and necessity of the students' abilities to accurately and effectively assess what their specific challenges and needs will be in a given academic situation. Whether it is recognizing vocabulary deficits, a lack of background knowledge, or the need to make-up for gaps in academic experiences, these students were highly adept at accurately assessing their situations and honestly gauging their assets, as well as where they may have been vulnerable. In doing this, and not underestimating the challenges they faced, these students expressed exceptional amounts of both humility and courage. Without this honest awareness, many of these students would not have done what was necessary for them to compete in academic worlds not built with them in mind.

SPOKE 2: THE STUDENT MANIFESTS AND/OR SEEKS OUT PROTECTIVE FACTORS THAT HAVE THE POTENTIAL TO OFFSET OR MITIGATE NEGATIVE EFFECTS OF THE RISK FACTORS.

An absolutely necessary correlate to Spoke 1 is the need to seek out assistance to address whatever needs may have been identified. Without this response, problems are addressed without potential solutions. Whether these solutions took the form of family members, teachers, personal habits, or structured programs, the student's ability and willingness to secure appropriate and effective responses to her/his needs allowed him/her to begin overcoming obstacles.

SPOKE 3: THE STUDENT MANAGES HER OR HIS PROTECTIVE FACTORS IN CONCERT TO PROPEL HER OR HIMSELF TOWARD HIGH ACADEMIC ACHIEVEMENT.

Given the scale of obstacles facing most of these students, the vast majority of them had to rely on *multiple* protective factors in order to excel. The students were often adept at strategically and simultaneously coordinating these resources in ways that helped them reach their academic goals. This coordination involved knowing when to utilize which resources, how to combine resources, and how/when to tap into the various aspects of the protective factors being implemented. Additionally, various groups, or *clusters* of protective factors that were particularly common and/or effective are included in here.

SPOKE 4: THE STUDENT RECOGNIZES THE EFFECTIVENESS OF THE PROTECTIVE FACTORS AND CONTINUES TO REFINE AND IMPLEMENT THEM.

As a means of encouraging their self-efficacy, these students consciously recognized the value and potency of their protective factors, which in turn motivated them to enhance and improve these factors to meet ongoing challenges. The acumen and awareness required to evaluate and assess efficacy played essential roles in helping these students excel. Here they are becoming fully convinced that what they do matters, and that they can greatly influence their own destiny.

SPOKE 5: THE CONSTANT AND CONTINUOUS REFINEMENT AND IMPLEMENTATION OF PROTECTIVE FACTORS, ALONG WITH THE EVOLVING VISION OF THE STUDENT'S DESIRED DESTINATION, SUSTAIN THE STUDENT'S PROGRESS.

The final spoke of the Cycle—not the "last" because like a metaphorical wheel the Cycle is essentially ongoing—emphasizes the resolute visions that the students have of where they see themselves upon completion of a particular academic task or journey. It is this vision, combined with the protective resources they have cultivated and nourished along the way, which sustains them, even when the inevitable obstacles appear along the way.

THE HUB (EMOTIONAL INTELLIGENCE) AND THE EFFECTIVE AND PURPOSEFUL MANAGEMENT OF EMOTIONS

If we speak of the steps of the Cycle as spokes, then there is a "hub" around which the spokes rotate and gain momentum. This hub is an amalgam of closely related self-management abilities including skillful and effective management of emotions amid stressful times, adeptness in social environments, impulse control and effective decision making under duress. The combined articulation of these basic characteristics can be found in the concept of *emotional intelligence,* popularized by Goleman (1995) in the psychology literature. Essentially the practical value of this emotional intelligence is that ultimately it works to facilitate effective utilization of available protective factors.

Furthermore, these emotional intelligence skills are of particular value to the potentially resilient students given the inordinate amount of stress, challenges, and obstacles under which most of them will find themselves throughout their academic careers. The five-spoke cycle only works because the students take active roles in managing them; this management is predicated on the development of this emotional intelligence skill set.

Primarily through use of actual narratives of the students, the practical reflection of the Cycle's hub and spokes are thoroughly explored, amplified, and supported in the following chapters. As the spokes are being discussed, references to identified "major" protective factors (from Appendix D) and the corresponding percentages of students who identified them are included parenthetically. "Major" was operationalized as at least 25% of the students in the study identifying them as crucial to their academic performance.

Chapter Four

The Cycle in Context:
Spoke 1 "Recognizing Reality"

SPOKE 1: THE STUDENT REALISTICALLY RECOGNIZES HER OR HIS MAJOR RISK FACTORS.

In order to truly appreciate the uniqueness and distance characterizing these students' academic and emotional journeys, the educational disparity in background and opportunities between these and middle class students must be reiterated. In fact 44/50 (88%) of the sample explicitly emphasized their own sub-par pre-college academic preparation as a major risk factor and psychological stressor (see Appendix E for complete listings psychological stressors).

As was presented earlier, the data overwhelmingly confirm that in a multitude of ways low socioeconomic, ethnic minority students are at a distinct disadvantage when it comes to competing academically. Generally speaking not only do these students come from under-funded, low performing schools, but they have limited access to academic role models within their communities and face both overt and subtle racism and discrimination on a regular basis. Additionally, many come from linguistically and culturally marginalized backgrounds, and therefore must overcome those barriers in order to excel in the classroom. In addition to these extraordinary challenges, they are exposed to infinitely more, as well as more injurious, social risk factors as compared to their wealthier, mostly white middle class peers.

The infamous litany of urban scourges: drugs, gangs, violence, poor health care, etc. are realities which must be dealt with on a daily basis. While the reality of this acute disadvantage does not control destiny, it does create a dynamic where excelling academically is not the norm, and as a result requires the effort and intervention of multiple stakeholders.

Because the socioeconomic and academic realities that these students face could not be ignored, overlooked, or minimized, an essential ingredient of their resilience was their exceptional ability to understand and articulate the realities of their situations. Often at early ages, most of these 50 resilient students exhibited the unique ability to identify and appreciate the difficult situations into which they were born and educated with a sincere understanding as to the challenges they would have to overcome. The vast majority (96%) exhibited this aptitude. Though sometimes painful, these realizations were essential in that they often propelled the students to take the necessary steps to make up for whatever they might have been missing. Consequently, in an important way these appraisal skills were closely connected with the students' crucial abilities to actively seek out invaluable protective resources.

The profundity of this realistic appraisal, as well as the students' proactive responses, cannot be overstated. Often these students were coming from severely disenfranchised educational backgrounds, and then, when entering prestigious academically rigorous high schools or colleges, they were being expected to compete head to head with academically and economically privileged classmates. As a result, very frequently these resilient students only truly appreciated the depth of the inequality to which they had been subjected when they were forced to compare themselves to these more privileged peers.

AWARENESS OF INEQUALITY: STUDENTS SPEAK

The most common time and place for this risk factor recognition dynamic was early in the students' high school or college careers. Thirty eight out of the fifty (76%) reported this recognition when they entered competitive high schools or colleges. These students often left educationally sub-par schools where they were academic standouts, only to find themselves in a new world where the possession of vast amounts of academic background knowledge and competencies was assumed.

Antonio's reflection of his freshmen year captures the students' need to "wakeup" to new realities and expectations:

When I got here (to college) I got frustrated. I knew that I was not going to be able to skate by like in high school. There (in his high school) all I had to do was study 20 minutes before the test, not give the teacher a hard time, and say "please" and "thank you" and compared to everyone else, I was a good student. At my first English comp class here, the teacher asked "Who read Plato in high school?" Almost the whole class raised their hands. I knew then I was in trouble, but once I accepted that, I was like OK; I need to get busy catching up to these guys. (Antonio, Hispanic Male, 20)

As is evident in Antonio's case, it was their ability to accept the situation for what it was, without getting defensive or angry, which allowed them to then address it effectively. Had Antonio fought the reality that he was under prepared, or had he engaged in denial by being too afraid to admit it to himself, then he never would have been able to overcome and progress.

Similarly, Santana's move from a New York City housing project to a relatively wealthy suburban high school captures the clash and accompanying self-doubt that can arise when these students are forced to confront the inequality of their educational backgrounds:

> Culture shock is the only word I can use to describe that experience. One day I was in the city with all my friends getting pastelitos at the corner bodega, the next I'm surrounded by rich White kids and I didn't know nobody. I also went from being the smartest kid in the class to just feeling clueless. I mean, everyone was really into school and college was a big deal, so it was really competitive . . . And they just kind of knew how to play the game. Sometimes I felt like they (the other students) had their own school language, they just knew how to speak it and I sure didn't. In comparison to them, I felt barely educated. It was a big change and I knew I would have to get my shit together. (Santana, Hispanic Male, 22).

Santana's dramatic clash, and the resulting humbling of his sense of academic readiness, is a stark example of how cultures and norms can diverge, as well as the fact that it is the marginalized student who will have to adapt to the academic expectations, and not vice versa.

The crucial part of the dynamic is not simply the students' acknowledgment of the acute challenges that lie ahead for them, but the willingness to address those challenges through action. Jasmine's reflection of entering her four year college after completing her two year associate's degree provides a glimpse into what can happen if the student refuses to acknowledge and accept academic disparities and respond accordingly:

> I was so full of myself because I got a scholarship . . . I thought that (the scholarship) meant that, you know, I belonged, that I was ready. I remember being in my European history class on the first day . . . the teacher was asking questions, like, What were the causes of World War I? And, How did the war affect the economy? stuff like that . . . I had *no* idea. I didn't even know who fought in that war, I thought it was verse Russia. But other people knew this stuff. And it was the first day, so it's not like they just learned it in this class, they knew it already . . . as like background knowledge . . . I got really heated (angry). I blamed the teacher, thinking that the questions were stupid. I even skipped the next class as like a protest. But stuff like that happened in my other classes too. It was like things came easier to the other students, like they just knew stuff, almost like an

inside joke. I tried to tell myself that it was no big deal, that the classes would be the same at county college (her previous school). But I couldn't keep fooling myself. After I got my first few grades back I knew that I was going to have to change my approach. I needed to keep a B average to keep my scholarship, and I was in trouble . . . Once I accepted that this was a new level, and that the same old effort and systems wouldn't work, things started to change. I committed to reading everything I could, asking lots of questions and going for extra help at the writing lab . . . these are things I never had to do before, but it was a new level. And if I wanted to stay I would have to. (Jasmine, African American Female, 22)

In Jasmine's case it becomes evident that there are several different reactions to the situation that students like her could have. As overwhelmed, academically insecure students often do, she could have continued to resist the reality that she had to play "academic catch up," and not changed her approach. But in situations where bright students with mediocre or sub-par educational backgrounds (like most of the students from this study) are attempting to excel in competitive environments, there is little time and room for denial, indecision or self-pity. If the students do not adapt quickly and decisively to new challenges, their situations could quickly spiral downward, and they could easily find themselves on the outside looking in.

In exploring this process of recognizing and reacting to the feelings of academic insecurity, these students often expressed their beliefs that the other students, presumably those from wealthier backgrounds and higher quality schools, did indeed have all of the educational background. As when Jasmine refers to it as an "inside joke," or Santana claims "Sometimes I felt like they had their own school language, they just knew how to speak it and I sure didn't" very often the resilient students truly believed that school was easy for the other students and that these presumably privileged peers magically possessed all of the requisite knowledge without much effort. Whether or not this was true in reality is almost beside the point. The fact that these resilient students *believed* it were true affected their academic self-images, and required that they deal with the reality of that perception.

It is important to make the distinction here between statistically probable outcomes when comparing the low socioeconomic ethnic minority students from this study with their wealthier, mostly white counterparts. Because the statistical reality for students like Jasmine, Santana and the rest is not to excel academically in academically rigorous environments, it is very easy for them to submit to inertia and join most of their community peers who have either barely finished high school and/or have dropped out of college. Again, social class differences are essential here. In contrast to their high socioeconomic peers, if the students in this study were to drop out of college and go into the work force, they would experience little, if any social stigma. They simply would be doing what most of their peers were doing and were expected to do. They may disappoint their parents, but most often there would not be shame or outrage. This reality makes the students' ability to recognize and react to their challenges even more audacious. In many ways, this willingness and ability to travel the road less taken lies at the heart of these students' resilient journeys.

While the primary focus here is on academics, it is important to note that this recognition and acceptance dynamic did not only revolve around educational deficits, but in a more general socioeconomic/cultural sense as well. These resilient students often reported incidents and anecdotes where they really began to understand and accept the depth of the disparity between themselves and middle class America. Whether is was memories of not having certain things, paltry Christmases, sharing rooms/beds with siblings, being afraid to walk down their streets at night, or in some extreme cases skipped meals, the students expressed anger, regret and bitterness over being born into difficult circumstances.

Very often this awareness mirrored Angel's description of his first trip to summer camp when he was ten years old:

> My first summer of day camp I didn't know what to expect. . . . My mom put me on the bus everyday and I would take like a 45 minute ride. We'd leave Newark and the scenery would change so dramatically. Our dirty hot streets would give way to trees, grass, and big clean houses. I remember watching kids my age playing in front of those houses, and slowly I began to realize that some people did live like on TV. . . . That summer was when I knew that we lived in the ghetto. (Angel, Hispanic Male, 20).

As with many of the students, it is only when Angel is exposed to life outside of his immediate neighborhood that he begins to gauge just how much he is missing.

Similarly, for Angel and others this understanding of disadvantage eventually evolved into a powerful form of motivation. As will be discussed in detail later in the text, the desire to move up in social and academic class is a primary motivator that increases in strength in proportion to the degree to which the student feels angry, disappointed, or bitter about their original socioeconomic standing.

Another significant theme evident in the experiences of these students related to recognizing challenges were issues of guilt and responsibility. While the students intellectually knew that their circumstances were not their fault, there was evidence that they did feel shame, responsibility and sometimes guilt over their circumstances.

A common occurrence reported by many students which evidences this shame was a reluctance to admit where they grew up or embarrassment for having grown up there. This would often manifest itself when students were away at college and the inevitable "Where are you from?" questions would arise. Jamal's recollection of his freshmen year captures this dynamic well:

> I hated telling people where I was from because there were so many stereotypes about it. When people hear Jersey City all they think about is gangs and violence and stuff, and I didn't want to be associated with that, especially when I first meet someone . . . I mean I wanted to fit in, to start with a clean slate, but it is like my past followed me. I know it is probably not good to say, but I was embarrassed about it, I wanted to be from a rich town and I wasn't . . . In a strange way, sometimes I felt like it was my fault that I was from there. I know it's dumb. But that's how I felt sometimes. (Jamal, African American Male, 19)

Like most of the students, Jamal knew intellectually that where he is from is not his fault, but he also knew that people did judge, and he did not want to be judged based on where he happened to be from. Like other students, Jamal looked at his low socioeconomic background as baggage which he would have to carry around.

Metacognition, Self-Evaluation, and Self-Control: Students Speak

As the previous section on emotional intelligence touched upon, two crucial abilities exhibited by these students were metacognition and honest self-evaluation. For our purposes, metacognition refers to the ability to analyze and understand one's own thought processes and patterns in ways that approximate reality; whereas, self-evaluation involves the ability to evaluate and assess oneself with honesty. To a certain extent, these closely related mental faculties are on display above as the students reflected on and evaluated their backgrounds, limitations, and challenges. However, even more explicit examples of these skills were evident in these students as they essential taught themselves how to study.

Generally speaking, the students in this study were not only highly adept at comprehending the *hows* and *whys* of their thought patterns and resulting actions, but they appreciated and counted on that ability at various points in their academic careers. One common arena in which these students showed extraordinary aptitude was in their capacity to design and develop efficacious study patterns and strategies that matched how their minds worked, their mental assets, and their academic contexts. Their prowess in this area was contingent upon their ability to be metacognitive and effectively evaluate themselves.

A common theme of the students' study habits is the presence of significant amounts of structure and discipline. Forty out of fifty (80%) developed
and explicitly valued specific study plans. For the most part these structures
were created and self-imposed in response to their own understandings of
their tendencies and their environments. Additionally, the students' awareness
of the significant hurdles they had to overcome, as discussed in detail earlier,
also played a role in these designs. Mario's stringent approach to exam preparation reflects this dynamic well:

> I was very aware of how much the odds were against me when I got to college. I
> had a lot of pressure on me and really wanted to do good . . . I also knew myself
> and that I was distracted easy . . . A lot of that came from where I grew up too.
> My house and my neighborhood were hectic, so I was like all over the place . . .
> I knew I had to structure my time really good. Especially with all the freedom that
> college gives you. I'm not good with too much time . . . I made sure to hit the
> books every morning and every night, and tried to keep it up no matter what . . . I
> also had this thing where I would pretend that the assignment was due three days
> before it actually had to be handed in. That way I had it done on time, even if I got
> distracted or something . . . that really worked for me. (Mario, Hispanic Male, 23)

Mario's strategies are clearly a product of his assessment of himself, as well
as his awareness of his own strengths and weaknesses. By understanding his
own propensity for distraction, he was able to create a rigorous study pattern
that kept him focused and completing his assignments on time.

While, like Mario, many students did rely on stringent and structured study
plans, others used their knowledge of themselves and specifically how they
learned best, in order to excel academically. Lucy in particular developed a
complex study plan based on linking her preferred learning styles to her academic tasks. In her description of her plan the high level of self-knowledge
these students often exhibited is clearly illustrated:

> I am a very visual person; I'm really good with images, pictures and graphs
> and stuff so I have learned that I have to use that no matter what I am learning.
> But while I am visual, I am not mathematical at all . . . I have always been lost
> in math class. I just don't grasp it. But because I know this about myself I can
> design good ways to study . . . Even with math, I try to make it as visual as
> possible. I draw lots of charts and graphs and use highlighters and stuff, and it
> works. (Lucy, Hispanic Female, 19)

Metacognition and Self Evaluation: Staying on Track

Perhaps even more valuable than using self-knowledge as tools for devel-
oping learning/study strategies has been these students' ability to use self-

knowledge as a way to stay on their academic paths despite constant and acute distraction. In order to more fully understand the importance and difficulty of staying on academic track, the degree to which these students are anomalies must be reiterated here. The majority of the time the academic paths that most of them have taken are in direct opposition to those of their community peers. Growing up poor and Black or Hispanic means that many of your peers, whether they be friends or family members, are not "A" students in high school and are not on their way to college. Many of them will struggle to make it through high school, have consistent run-ins with the law, have children as teenagers, and then raise their children in the same neighborhood in which they were raised. Given this reality, a vital task for the students in this study has been to use their knowledge of themselves to develop the self-discipline to withstand the potent forces that may potentially pull them off track. This is where key protective factors discussed in more detail later, namely *persistence* (94%), *a strong future orientation* (86%), and *self-motivation* (86%) play major roles.

Marcus's philosophy clearly reflects the value of self-knowledge in helping to keep these students on track, even as risk factors consistently reveal themselves:

> In my freshman philosophy class our final project was to write our own life philosophy using all the stuff we learned in the class. I thought that class was going to be boring, but it turned out to be pretty cool, because like my teacher said, philosophy is really about creating a code for your life . . . the two main philosophers I used were Socrates and Kant. . . . Socrates' main thing was "know thyself" meaning that you have to be really in-touch with yourself and your feelings, and Kant's big thing was self-determination, like making sure that you control your life and not others . . . that's really important to me, because coming from where I came, there's so much that could mess me up, I mean, all I have to do is look around and I can see so much of what *not* to do and where I *don't* want to be. (Marcus, African American Male, 26)

Like many of the students, Marcus recognizes the importance of using self-knowledge and self-determination for the specific purpose of avoiding potential environmental risk factors and pitfalls.

A primary pitfall that often had to be avoided was the effect of negative peer groups. In Lamar's words below the need to resist falling prey to group norms in order to fit in is articulated well:

> It was really important for me not let other people's views of what it means to be cool or manly influence what I do . . . it sounds easy, but if you are not on top of things you can easily get sucked in. Where I grew up it was considered soft or

girly to get good grades in school . . . there were guys who would actually fail
on purpose! I know is sounds crazy, but that is how much pressure there was to
fit in. And fitting in really meant not caring, "just chillin," being laid back . .
. But I knew that that would backfire in the end. Those guys who were cool in
high school are nothing now. They're hanging out on the corner or locked up.
(Lamar, African American Male, 20)

As with most adolescents, there existed a natural tendency for the students
from this study to follow the in-crowd and to emulate the "cool" kids. However, in anti-academic environments like those that many of these students
grew up in there are powerful forces pulling them away from achievement and
often ostracizing those who do achieve. As Lamar articulates, if you are not
both aware of this possibility and willing to take steps to avoid it, the results
can be ruinous.

The Power of Honest Reflection

In reviewing these students' reflections, the amount of honesty as well as the
degree of sincerity characterizing their assessments, appears to have played a
crucial role in their academic success. Given the size and number of hurdles
they had to face it was very important that these students did not fool themselves into believing that massive effort and discipline would not be required.
If they had not been able to honestly and realistically assess where they were,
and what it would take to progress, then it is very likely that they would not
have been prepared for the awesome challenge.

In essence, these students have been able to avoid a well established common obstacle to achievement for non-resilient low socioeconomic students,
namely the *attitude achievement paradox*. The attitude achievement paradox
posits that low-income youth often have ignorance induced unrealistically
high academic and career objectives and lack an understanding as to exactly
what meeting those objectives would actually entail. As a result of this self-
delusion, when they are actually faced with the process of pursuing their
objectives they are completely unprepared, quickly become discouraged, and
subsequently give up. Because the students in this study were extremely adept
at realistically assessing their situations, their strengths, and their weaknesses,
they were able to avoid this sad phenomenon. For example, when Antonio,
Santana, and Jasmine are hit with the realization that they have catching up
to do, they do not pretend it is no big deal or exhibit denial behavior. On the
contrary, they assess the situation and respond accordingly.

The above descriptions of these students' tendencies to realistically ap-
praise their challenges and to adapt themselves to new academic expectations
do not in anyway intend to blame them for often being under-prepared, nor

do they assume that the students do not bring significant strengths to the table as well. On the contrary, these students bring incredible gifts and experiences with them and have built off of those assets. However, the fact remains that when marginalized or disenfranchised students attempt to excel in mainstream environments, they are the ones who must learn, adjust, and configure themselves to the new academic culture. Never is it the other way around.

It is not that the students' backgrounds are inherently weak, it is simply that there is a severe disconnect between these students' backgrounds and that which is valued by the academic milieu. Ultimately, what this means is that the students had to add many academic skills, norms and values to what they already knew and experienced. As a result, in many ways they end up being enriched and more able than their wealthier peers to know and relate to a wider variety of peoples.

This chapter is focused on Spoke 1 of the Resilience Cycle "The student realistically recognizes her or his major risk factors," thus it primarily describes the students' adeptness at interpreting their worlds and consequently the risk factors with which they must deal. However, as illustrated above, the value of this adeptness is not in the realizations themselves, but rather in the students' abilities and willingness to use those realizations to procure effective protective factor resources. This leads directly to Spoke 2: "The student manifests and/or seeks out protective factors that have the potential to offset or mitigate negative effects of the risk factors" where a more detailed look at the actual protective factors utilized by the students during their academic careers will be presented and explored.

Chapter Five

The Cycle in Context: Spoke 2 "Manifesting Help"

SPOKE 2: THE STUDENT MANIFESTS AND/OR SEEKS OUT PROTECTIVE FACTORS THAT HAVE THE POTENTIAL TO OFFSET OR MITIGATE NEGATIVE EFFECTS OF THE RISK FACTORS.

Spoke 2 is focused on the essential ability to respond to perceived risk with appropriate protective factors. Protective factors are essentially resources that students exploit in order to achieve. As in Appendix D, they are often categorized as being either dispositional (personality characteristics/proclivities/ tendencies), familial (direct support from immediate or extended family members), and environmental (support from schools, teachers, community members, programs, etc.). This categorization is done with the full realization that such categories are somewhat artificial, and that many of the protective factors can easily bleed into more than one category. However, for the purposes of both clarity and analysis these categories have proven effective.

SELF-RELIANCE: THE VALUE OF DISPOSITION

Interestingly, and perhaps surprisingly, in conducting this research dispositional protective factors were both most commonly identified and emphasized by the students themselves. In fact, the top five most frequently cited protective factors were dispositional (*Desire/willingness to class jump- 94%, Persistence-94%, Sense of Obligation to Family- 94%, High-Self Esteem-92%, and Internal Locus of Control- 92%*). While it is virtually impossible to separate students' dispositions from their exposure to environmental factors and familial influences, and these dispositional attributes are often a result of important environmental and familial resources, what is clear is that from the students' perspectives, these personality traits/habits were of paramount importance. Furthermore, what the above common dispositional factors all have in common is that they are premised on the notion of self-reliance.

Whether or not this emphasis on self-reliance is ultimately a positive or negative can be debated. However, it is clear that on some level these students have bought into the idea that ultimately they are responsible for what happens to them. This self-reliance theme is prevalent even though these students simultaneously emphasize the absolute value of their environmental and familial resources. These seemingly contradictory belief systems were evident in many of the students' narratives.

The following quotes illustrate the students' rhetorical support for self-reliance on one hand and their appreciation of the crucial roles that other factors have played on the other:

It's all about what you do, the decisions you make. I knew that no one was going to do it for me, that it was up to me to get it done, that's just the way it is . . . I had the will to achieve and I had to do it alone. . . . My mother was everything to me, without her I would not be here (in college). She taught me about hard work and sacrifice first hand, through example. Without her I would be like my friends growing up, either dead, in jail, or in the military. (Sean, African American Male, 19)

I think the most important thing that has helped me be a good student was my own desire to get ahead, to get a college education. . . . That's the difference between me and the dropouts, I think that I just want it more and am willing to work. I lot of them are lazy . . . Without my scholarship I wouldn't have been able to go to college; maybe community college, but definitely not here. My family had no money, and they weren't about to take out a big loan. When I got that scholarship I was filled with hope, it was like a sign from God. (Irene, Hispanic, Female 18)

Throughout the student narratives there are multiple examples of these sorts of seemingly contradictory assertions. In discussing these discrepancies with the students, it becomes clear that often these ambiguities reflect their own uncertainty as to exactly how and why they have excelled academically. In a sense this should be expected. Like most people, prior to this research initiative and the accompanying interviews, these students have not been forced to think systematically about how they got where they are academically. Nor have they been probed and prodded about their thoughts on the topic. Thus when they respond to questions they are engaging in a somewhat spontaneous form of metacognitive reflection and analysis pertaining to their academic careers. Consequently, their spontaneity may account for some of the ambivalence evident.

Another possible reason for the students' apparent over emphasis on their own dispositional protective factors is their maturity levels and the fact that at the time of the interviews they were all in the *process* of reaching their academic and professional goals, thus they may not have been certain about the significance of all of the contributing factors.

Pertinent to this issue is research done on a smaller subset of this population titled *Academic Resilience in Retrospect: Following up a Decade Later* (Morales, 2008). As the title implies, this research re-interviewed resilient students after ten years. One of the findings was that these students placed much more emphasis on the assistance they received from others in the follow-up interviews as compared with their initial ones. As these students reached their academic and professional goals and increased in both experiences and maturity, they were able to reflect more, and often gave much more credit to others while taking less credit for themselves.

The following sections focus more on environmental and familial protective factors that these students utilized in the process of their resilience.

STRATEGIC SEEKING

What was especially unique about these students is that they were able to actively seek out *appropriate and suitable* resources, even at relatively young ages. They were able to do this because of their perspicacity and their willingness to acknowledge need and reach out for assistance. Often the protective factors they procured were especially suitable to their particular challenges or needs. This ability is a necessary post-requisite for the resilient student. Without this, the acknowledgement of limitations or academic deficiencies (Spoke 1) would be the end of the journey, as it often is for many non-resilient students. Once one knows one's limitations and disadvantages, one must also be willing and able to address them in purposeful and effective ways.

The students' interpersonal skills and personal affects often served as a prerequisite to attracting many of these valuable protective factors, particular social capital, which came in the form of supportive teachers/professors, community members, etc. As discussed in the previous "Hub" section on emotional intelligence, students who are likeable, positive, and energetic tended to attract assistance.

While a complete list of protective factors can be found in Appendix D, among the most frequently cited were: Dispositional Factors- *Persistence* 47 (94%), *Sense of Obligation to One's Family* 47 (94%), *High Self-esteem* 46 (92%), *and Internal Locus of Control* 46 (92%); Environmental Factors- *Caring k–12 School Personnel* 45 (90%), *State/Federally Funded College Bridge Programs* 44 (88%), and *Attendance at a "Non-neighborhood/Zoned" School* 36 (72%). Familial Protective Factors- *Authoritative Parenting Styles* 41 (82%), *Parental Expectations Demonstrated by Words and Actions* 40 (80%), and *Mother Modeling a Strong Work Ethic* 37 (74%). This wide array of varied protective factors speaks to the variety of risk factors that these students must overcome (more on use of multiple protective factors can be found in the discussion of Spoke 3).

AFFABILITY AND ENDEARMENT: STUDENTS SPEAK

A primary dispositional protective factor that allowed many of the crucial environmental protective factors to manifest themselves was the students' affability 39 (78%). Within the context of this study, affability refers to one's ability to endear oneself to others and the state of being where others are drawn to one. Basically, when we speak of those who are affable, we are speaking of those who attract concern and attention. And while most of these students did not actually use the word "affable" they did speak explicitly about behaviors and attitudes that fit with our definition of the term.

Latisha's description of the advice that her mother gave her sums up what many of these students reported in relation to the value and importance of affability:

One of my mother's favorite sayings was "You can catch more flies with honey than with vinegar" and to me that meant to be nice if you want to get people to help you. Now, like my mama said, this ain't always easy cause some times you don't want to be all nice and everything, but in the end its best for you if can. (Latisha, African American female, 20)

An interesting phenomenon which is hinted at in Latisha's words, but more evident in some of the other African American students' narratives is that this need to smile for others, even if you don't really feel like it, has a particular history within African American culture. Most notably, historically slaves often had to have "two faces," a real one for each other, and then the fake smile for the White people. This phenomenon appears to have found its way into some of these students' mindsets. Jamal's understanding of interpersonal dynamics articulates this reality well:

> As Black people I think it is harder to be all nice to White people because there is always this feeling like they are the enemy, so why should I be nice? I know it doesn't really make sense on the surface, but it is more just like a feeling. My first reaction is to be like defensive and closed around White people. . . . But I have learned over the years that they have a lot of power, so if I don't pull them in, I am just hurting myself. (Jamal, African American Male, 19)

Jamal's thoughts connect to another important issue. If we think back to how many of these students have grown up, their being highly affable can be viewed as somewhat unexpected. One of the established consequences of growing up in low-income urban environments is that due to the need for self-protection, it often increases cynicism, suspicion, and ultimately defensiveness. These qualities are in direct opposition to affability because they engender a pulling-back away from others, even if those others can be helpful. Furthermore, because affability is often a prerequisite to capitalizing on potentially helpful others, this quality is especially valuable.

Lucy's description of her neighborhood illustrates this dynamic well:

> Weakness is just not something you could show where I grew up. Even the girls were ready to fight all the time. So you develop a way of being which is like being cool, like nothing bothers you, no matter what. You carry this "whatever" attitude . . . it's like a shield because it can protect you from being exposed. (Lucy, Hispanic Female, 21)

In Lucy's narrative we see this sense of detachment which characterized how many of these students were socialized in their home environments. However, in order to attract help, they often had to overcome this tendency that, while being well suited to the street, is not helpful in trying to excel academically. Dante's narrative demonstrates how this transformation often took place:

> I was a pretty bad kid in middle school. I had a really bad attitude with teachers and stuff, but I think that was because of where I lived. Especially as a boy, it was like I was supposed to be tough, and that meant disrespecting the teachers, not listening, all that stupid stuff . . . During eighth grade I was suspended 3 times. It was amazing I wasn't kicked out . . . Once I started getting serious about school and the idea that I wanted to go to college I knew that I was going to need help. . . . Nobody in my family, not even cousins or nothing have been to college, so who was I going to ask for help? I mean, my mom is a cleaning woman who barely got through 8th grade. . . . So the first person I targeted was my guidance

counselor because she had these beautiful posters on her walls of these green college campuses, and I was thinking, yea, that's where I need to go . . . She was an older white women that nobody really liked, but I knew I needed her . . . I decided to charm her because I thought that I needed as much attention from her as I could get. I made a bunch of appointments and always kept them. She would tell me how many kids would not show, so I made sure not to do that. I always said "please" and "thank you" and was like a real gentleman with her . . . that ended up being like the best thing I ever did . . . she helped me fill out the applications, talked to me about financial aid, and she even proofread my essay, which she said she wasn't supposed to do. I ended up getting a great scholarship . . . without her I may be in college, but I probably wouldn't be here and I would definitely be deep in debt. (Dante, African American Male, 19)

Dante's narrative is rich with themes that were common to many of the students in the study. First, we see that he had to defy what seemed to be the norm in his environment (namely being antagonistic toward the school and teachers) in order to begin moving toward his academic goal. The fact that he, (as well as many of the other students in the study), was able to recognize the negative consequences of his behavior at such a young age is notable. This requires a precocious self-awareness which is both valuable and unique. He was then able to target a specific protective factor (his guidance counselor) that was uniquely qualified to meet the needs created by his socioeconomic status (namely the lack of college graduates in his familial environment). Again, the fact that he was conscious about this decision speaks to a unique level of psycho-social awareness. Finally, he was able to present himself in an affable manner in order to engender special attention from his guidance counselor. He expanded his social network by using his exceptional interpersonal skills.

CULTIVATING SOCIAL AND CULTURAL CAPITAL

Like Dante, in recognizing their deficiencies, many of the students sought out human assets in order to increase their social capital. Social capital is a term popularized by Coleman (1990) and refers to access to people with insider knowledge of how to thrive within higher level social systems. This includes familiarity of appropriate linguistic styles, cultural expectations, and concrete knowledge on how to be successful. A related concept is Bourdieu's (1977) cultural capital, which is symbolic wealth that comes with being middle class, and which connect benefits to one's social class. From an educational achievement perspective—cultural capital refers to values and experiences common to upper-middleclass cultures that are highly valuable in formal school settings.

Because these students recognized that the social networks and cultural traditions they had were not especially valued by formal educational settings, they reached out and secured social and cultural capital from others.

To provide a sense of the variety of ways this process worked, several brief extant examples in are provided.

During his mid-adolescence Ricardo began spending more time at his church precisely so that he could get closer with a pastor whom he found particularly engaging. He volunteered to help out after services, joined the church's youth group, and had extended ecumenical conversations with the pastor. In the process, the pastor began to serve as Ricardo's spiritual advisor. So important was the pastor to Ricardo, that Ricardo describes him as almost singularly responsible for transforming him from class clown to serious and dedicated student.

During high school Crystal joined a women's mentoring program sponsored by a Wall Street brokerage firm explicitly so that she could gain contacts to a corporate world that was completely foreign to her. The result was a summer internship which she then parlayed into a part-time job. Crystal stayed in-touch with her mentor throughout college, worked at the firm during summers and breaks, and was offered a permanent position upon graduation from college.

Julie became highly engaged with her college student activities board and very close with the dean of students. As a result, the dean helped get her a graduate assistantship at a top state university where Julie ended up pursuing a graduate degree in college student personnel administration. Because of the graduate assistantship she was able to attend full-time and have her tuition covered.

In each of the above cases, the students put themselves in positions to ingratiate themselves to individuals who where in positions to provide them with unique and valuable access to tools of social ascension. Whether these tools are spiritual advisement and role modeling, corporate access, or academic opportunity they are especially important because, given the students socio-economic backgrounds, more often than not the individual providing the tool would not normally be part of the student's world had they not been sought out. It is important to note that these important social resources were not family members, cousins, or friends of the family as they often are for more wealthy people.

A look at the entire sample's identified protective factors bares this out. In looking at the significantly influential people who were able to provide the students with cultural and social capital, 90% of the students identified *Caring School Personnel (k–12)* and 70% identified *Caring School Personnel (College)*. In contrast, if we look at how many of the students identified family members as significant contributors of social and cultural capital, the closest we see is that 46% identified siblings as *Academic Role Models/ Trailblazers*. This is not intended to dismiss the value of their families. On the contrary, as discussed earlier *82%* valued their parents' *Authoritative Parenting Style*, 80% identified *High Parental Expectations Supported by Words and Actions* as crucial, and 74% identified their *Mothers' Modeling of Strong Work Ethic* as an essential component of their resilience. However, when it came to accessing valued insider connections to academic and professional worlds, their families simply were not a primary source. Consequently, these students recognized this reality, and took steps to address it.

Though her highly developed consciousness and articulation of the phenomenon is a bit unusual, Rosa's take on the need to reach beyond the immediate family and environment illustrates what many of these students have expressed and demonstrated . . . my home is my home, it's my world, but I am not stupid. I know that it is called the ghetto for a reason, its not a place I want to be long term . . . the word my Soc. (sociology) teacher uses is "marginal," like on the outside having to look in. . . . I realized fast that if I wanted to join that inside world, that middleclass world that I would have to find people that live in that world and can open it up to me. . . . It's not that I have to forget about my world or diss (disrespect) it, it's just that I need to access the world I want to enter, for me and my future kids. (Rosa, Hispanic Female, 21)

Spoke 2 of the Resilience Cycle is relatively simple, but profound at the same time. It is about generating the courage and acumen required to acknowledge one's needs, and then exposing oneself during the process of reaching out to get the "right" kind of help. This exposure makes one inherently vulnerable, but it is a necessary risk. Without these protective factors, these students would not have been able to overcome the odds that they had. However, what should be made clear is that because the mountains that these students must climb are so large and treacherous, one special protective factor is never enough. Consequently, these students have become highly adept at *orchestrating* multiple protective factors simultaneously. This is the essence of Spoke 3.

Chapter Six

The Cycle in Context:
Spoke 3 "Synthesizing Resources"

SPOKE 3: THE STUDENT MANAGES HER OR HIS PROTECTIVE FACTORS IN CONCERT TO PROPEL HER OR HIMSELF TOWARD HIGH ACADEMIC ACHIEVEMENT.

As briefly discussed earlier, what is often lost when simply identifying protective factors is an understanding of, and appreciation for, the process (*how* the protective factor results in the positive outcome) and the specific *relationships* between and among the various protective as well as risk factors. These areas have been among the least researched phenomena within the field of academic resilience. Consequently, this chapter covering Spoke 3 is especially comprehensive and detailed.

To truly value the importance of the protective factor resources discussed, it helps to be reminded of the dire circumstances into which many of these students have been born. A multitude of them managed to excel in school while confronting homelessness; physical, verbal and sexual abuse; absence of one or both parents (or drug addicted parents who may as well be absent); severe poverty; undiagnosed learning disabilities; barely functioning schools (which often had to be taken over by state authorities); language barriers; both blatant and subtle racism; depressed and violent communities; and all the suffocating toxicity that emanates from these situations. These are all on top of the "normal" stresses inherent to surviving adolescence even under the best of circumstances.

Understanding the depth, complexity, and comprehensiveness of risk that many of these students face, it becomes apparent why one or two valuable protective factors could never be enough. No matter how special the teacher, how committed the student, or how supportive the family, it takes multiple effective protective factors working in concert in order to propel these students toward overcoming the acute disadvantage which characterizes their beginnings. This symphony is at the core of Spoke 3: *The student manages her or his protective factors in concert to propel her or himself toward high academic achievement.*

In order to address this issue thoroughly, this chapter includes a variety of subsections all exploring how various protective factors and dynamics coalesced to engender academic resilience.

From the students' narratives, we have identified trends of temporal relationships between the protective factors and student progress that capture their interactions. Based on this protective factor framework, this chapter will identify the key protective factors cited by these resilient students, focus on the specific contextual process of how the factors resulted in success, and present trends of when, and in what combination, the protective factors appeared optimal. This unique approach presents a more authentic understanding of the protective factors and processes common to resilient student experiences.

The following sections attempt to group the protective factors into the most common formations resulting from students' reports of their experiences. The sections also demonstrate the symbiotic, interdependent, and temporal nature of the protective factors in context and how they result in the process know as academic resilience. First, we begin with two salient protective factor combinations (or "clusters") that produced resilience; we then focus on especially important protective factors "Intellectual Curiosity and Self motivation" and "Bicultural Selves." We then culminate with a closer look at strength based approaches to academic success, which includes a presentation of differentiated strengths and processes bases on racial and ethnic backgrounds.

PROTECTIVE FACTOR COMBINATION/CLUSTER #1: "IT'S OKAY TO BE SMART": SKILLFUL MENTORING FOR FUTURE SUCCESS

Protective Factors: Willingness/Desire to Class Jump, Caring School Personnel (k–12 and College), and a Strong Future Orientation

Willingness and Desire to Class Jump (94%) was characterized as the students' explicit longing to move up in social class, and in their acceptance of their perception of what it might mean to change social classes. While this may appear to be a simple conviction requiring little emotional or intellectual effort, often the contrary was the case. This is an area where the dynamics are significantly different for majority versus minority students. There is often a de facto consequence built into minority students that joining the middle class is a form of treason and/or "selling out." Therefore, before a student could fully commit to "class jumping" often he or she had to be coached and coaxed into doing so by a mentor, usually a caring school personnel member.

Effective caring school personnel were identified by many of the students in this study (K–12, 90% and college, 72%). These individuals (academic mentors) were described with words such as "encouraging," "empathetic," "supportive," "rigorous" and "down" ("down" is slang for understanding of youth culture and trustworthy). Additionally, the important mentors were in possession of cultural capital essential to students' success in moving from one milieu (low income/working class environments of color) to another (traditionally middle class, white, academic environments). In this manner, they often served as effective "cultural translators" literally and figuratively translating the language of academia into words and ideas that the students could readily understand. While this has proven true for virtually all of the students in this study who identified mentors as important, there was another essential role reported that these caring teachers and administrators played that rarely receives attention in the resilience/mentoring literature: that of convincing the students that it was indeed "okay" to commit to moving up in class.

While the specific approaches of persuasion differed, a common theme was that the school mentors would acknowledge the students' ambivalence, then reassure them that "moving up" did not necessarily mean a complete break from everything and everyone that they were used to, nor did it have to mean they become a new person. Additionally, they reminded those students who felt a strong obligation to their race and communities of origin (68%) that far from selling out, their success would actually put them in a more powerful position to do more for their families (both current and future) and their communities.

Dante's description of his college counselor is representative of what many of the students described:

> Part of me was tied to the 'hood' and didn't want to let that go. To be Black, to be truly Black meant that you were part of the struggle and that you did things in a "Black way." Whether it be how you speak, your music, your dress, you're distinguishing yourself from the White world. It's a form of resistance. I don't mean to get too political, but when you listen to guys like Cornell West or even Tupac, you can see what I'm talking about. . . . So I was into "Hip Hop," which isn't just rapping, it's a lifestyle, and the better I did in school and then going to college, more and more I felt like I would have to give that up, and that didn't feel right . . . But when I met Mr. Jackson (college counselor), he noticed that resistance . . . He broke it down for me. He was into Cornell West too, and he

asked me, is Cornell a sell out? And of course he is not, he's the Man. And who has more letters after his name than him? You see. So he showed me being intellectual and getting degrees doesn't have to mean selling out. It's about what you do when you get ahead, not just getting ahead. Cornell got his letters (academic degrees) and made change from there. (Dante, African American Male, 19)

Like many of the students in the study, Dante's reconciliation of academic success with his racial/ethnic community allegiance helped free him from resisting his achievement.

Another benefit of this freedom was that it helped students like Dante keep from sabotaging their own success. Given the common presence of a sense of obligation to one's race and class group prevalent in poorer communities of color, self-sabotage is often a disproportionably common phenomenon there. As part of this process, students sometimes, either consciously or subconsciously, do things to thwart their own success in order to keep themselves from leaving their peer group and having to join the dominant majority. Perhaps the most common phenomenon of this type is the student who fails on purpose to maintain acceptance by their peer group.

For the resilient students in this study however, reports of self-sabotage were relatively rare (38% of males and 12% of females). It can be logically surmised that these relatively low percentages are a result of the stratified set that makes the group. These students are all relative high achievers; therefore it can be assumed that students with significant self-sabotage issues would not have achieved enough to be included. However, for the students in the study for whom self-sabotage was an issue, the presence of the mentors played important roles. When the students' mentors convinced the students to be comfortable with this transition to academia, the students' propensity for self-sabotage decreased.

In addition to the willingness and ability to class jump, another dispositional protective factor tied to mentorship was the students' possession of a *strong future orientation*. A strong future orientation is characterized by thoughts, speech and behavior patterns that emphasize attainment of *prospective* goals and *potential* resources and outcomes, rather than immediate gratification and concerns. Eighty-six percent of the students in this study stressed future orientation as a significant protective factor. And while this dispositional attribute existed for most of the students prior to the mentors' interaction described earlier, it became considerably more prevalent and intense once the student became comfortable with the prospect of class jumping. Thus, often the academic mentors' primary role was to convince the students (either directly or indirectly) that positive ideas about the future were indeed realistic, attainable, and worthy.

Similar to the sabotage matter above, it can be inferred that the students who have met the requisite criteria for this study will generally posses significantly

Chapter Six

high levels of future orientation. However, as the students move through their college careers, planning for the future became a major concern for them. They reported a great deal of anxiety over the future, and expressed their gratitude for the mentors' guidance in this area (interestingly, female students were significantly more concerned with their professional futures and focused much more on preparation than males).

Through interaction with caring school personnel (particularly during the college years) the students received guidance, information, and confidence necessary to decrease stress and begin their planning. Because the students felt at ease with their position as college students, and because they received the support and approval they needed from their mentors, their futures became more known and less frightening.

As in Lourdes' case discussed earlier, we not only see the mentor helping smooth out the emotional and financial process of going to graduate school, and thus virtually securing a position in the middle class, but we also see a clear example of the mentor's provision of both cultural and social capital. The mentor had firsthand knowledge of how academia and graduate schools operate. This is knowledge that Lourdes' mother simply did not possess. By providing Lourdes' with this "insider knowledge" Miss. Carson is in effect compensating for Lourdes' family's lack of knowledge about academic matters, and providing Lourdes with a path toward her academic and professional goals. This knowledge also decreases the amount of stress and anxiety that Lourdes feels. When Lourdes refers to Miss. Carson as her "go to girl" this lifting of stress becomes apparent. When Lourdes talked about Miss Carson a smile took over her face and she appeared to actually exhale.

While the mentors have played other roles which will be explored later in this chapter, their general effectiveness in serving as physical, emotional, and intellectual bridges, linking the students to their futures, proved essential for these students.

PROTECTIVE FACTOR COMBINATION/CLUSTER #2 "SMILING YOUR WAY THROUGH SCHOOL": MAXIMIZING AVAILABLE RESOURCES

Help Seeking Tendencies, Affability, Optimism, State/Federally Funded College Bridge Programs, Caring School Personnel, College Clubs and Organizations, School Sponsored Tutoring

Perhaps the most clearly supplemental and facilitative symbiotic relationships appeared between dispositional protective factors that can be categorized as "proactive"- (i.e. *Help Seeking Tendencies* (82%), *Affability* (78%), and Optimism (64%)), as well as crucial environmental protective factors (i.e. *State/Federally Funded College Bridge Programs* (88%), *College Clubs and Organizations* (66%), *Caring School Personnel* (90%), and *School Sponsored Tutoring Services* (66%)). These two categories of protective factors are highly interdependent in that in order to maximize the latter, you must possess significant degrees of the former.

It was evident throughout that these students maintained optimistic and amiable personas and used those characteristics in order to draw help into their lives. What was surprising was the degree to which many of the students were not only aware of their ability to attract help, but were actually proud of it.

Sharita's metaphor of "putting people in her pocket" describes both the process and pride that many of these students felt when recruiting their educational helpers:

> My father used to always say "It's not what you know, it's who you know" . . . I think its good to know things, but in school, especially college, it's like political. We (African Americans) don't have the same type of contacts as White folks, but we should. . . . Knowing people can help you get over or just get help with things . . . when I applied for a job at in the computer lab, which is like the perfect job everybody wants because you are right there (on campus) and you can do your homework while you work, they needed college references and I had like five people here at the college to put down. And I think that's what got me the job. I had a lot of people who could support me . . . I've always been good at putting people in my pocket, that's like getting people on my side, that way, when I need them, there they are. All ready. (Sharita, African American Female, 22)

The enthusiasm with which Sharita speaks about her available social capital was not unique to her. Many students spoke excitedly and almost boastfully about the people that they had "put in their pockets."

What was perhaps even more unexpected than their pride and enthusiasm was the calculating aspect of their interactions with potential helpers. As the students grew older, they became more and more aware of their need and desire to enlist others. This was not done in a manipulative or exploitive manner; the students knew that there were caring personnel available and that those people liked to help. The students were simply taking advantage of the situation.

Part of their understanding of the need and importance for getting others on their side was their awareness as to how their personalities and affect helped to draw others in. Many students were aware that by being pleasant, talkative, and outgoing, they were more likely to ingratiate themselves to others.

Nestor's beginning of the semester routine was more strategic than most, but captures both the planned nature and means by which the students solicited important people:

> At the beginning of each semester I would gather my syllabuses and look at all the professors' office hours. I would then make it a point to stop by and see them during the first couple of weeks *before* I really needed anything. I'd stop in smile, and ask some basic question . . . they love that. They'd be like "nobody ever comes to my office hours, I am so glad you are here!" That way, if I did get into trouble or needed something from their class, they knew who I was and would want to help. Even simple stuff like with tests. You'd be surprised how much they would tell you about what's gonna be in the test when you just talk to them one on one. (Nestor, Age 21, Hispanic American)

The students' highly developed interpersonal skills were a key in increasing the degree to which others offered their assistance. Additionally, though the dynamics were more complex and intricate, these skills helped the students maximize other important environmental resources, namely the *State/Federally Funded College Bridge Programs* (88%), *the College Clubs and Organizations* (66%), *and School Sponsored Tutoring Services* (66%).

The *State/Federally Funded College Bridge Programs* helped support the students in four major ways: by alleviating significant portions of the financial burdens of college attendance, by providing students with a familiar community within the non-familiar college setting, by alleviating many of the major insecurity stressors identified by the students, and by providing a structure through which the students could both use and refine the dispositional protective factors discussed throughout the text.

It is important to note that forty-four of the fifty students (88%) were participants in one form or another of these programs, and 100% of these students identified the programs as a major protective factor for them. These programs come in several different names and forms. In terms of state programs, in New Jersey the programs are called EOP (Educational Opportunity Program) at private higher education institutions and EOF (Educational Opportunity Fund) at public ones. In New York, the programs are HEOP (High Education Opportunity Program) and EOP (Education Opportunity Program) respectively.

While the programs have slightly different funding formulas and organizational structures, their shared goal is to help economically disadvantaged youth to achieve academically at the collegiate level. Common important elements of these programs include a summer bridge program designed to acclimate students to college life prior to their the official start of their freshman year and build a sense of community, counseling and academic advising to help students make the emotional and academic transition from high school to college, and financial support to help cover tuition, books, and living expenses.

It is essential to point out here that while the students in this study have placed a great deal of emphasis on dispositional protective factors such as persistence, locus of control, and self-motivation, without well-funded, well designed government supported initiatives such as these, those individually based personal qualities would not have produced such exceptional results. Without this type of scaffolding supporting the students' journeys, few if any would make it to the extent that they have. Furthermore, while resilience research has often been accused of focusing too much on individual effort and, not enough on government support initiatives, it must be stated that one without the other is of little use. They have been mutually essential for the students in this study.

Perhaps not surprisingly, the financial assistance aspect of these programs has had a direct and profound benefit on student achievement. Given the infamously exorbitant (and growing) costs of higher education in America, without financial assistance these students would not be where they are. In speaking with the students about this issue, a common theme reported by many was that while they probably would have made it into some higher education institution without the financial benefit of these programs, they would be at less prestigious institutions, would be there part time while working, would not be able to dorm and/or would have the stress of massive loans waiting for them upon graduation.

Each of these alternatives individually has been determined to decrease college persistence rates, taken together they create a series of risks that would serious diminish the likelihood of success for most students, regardless of their individual will, determination and effort.

The value of the sense of community created by these bridge programs cannot be overstated, especially given the severe cultural discontinuity often evident between the student and the college. Time and time again the students talked about the sense of community created by the programs and how that community served to decrease the culture shock they had to face. Because these programs are majority minority and by definition serving only lower SES students, there is an immediate comfort level experienced by the students. Additionally, because these programs invite the students onto campus the summer before their freshmen year when few others are on campus, the end effect is to shrink the campus so as to provide a sense of intimacy. This intimacy provides these atypical students with a social support group prior to the arrival of throngs of students in late August.

The following series of quotes are descriptions of students' appreciation of that initial sense of community:

During that summer I got my posse together . . . We were like a fraternity because we all were from the same types of neighborhoods, we were all Black and Latino, it was like so comfortable. So we all hung out . . . When September came I had no trouble going back (to the college) I was actually looking forward to it. (Denise, African American Female, 21)

EOP (the Educational Opportunity Program) became my second home. All of my friends now I met then . . . I'm a really shy person. Like, I'm really good one on one, but I am bad in groups. I just get quiet. This was why I was so scared about going away to college, I had never slept outside of my apartment, and here I was set to go to this scary place called "college." All I could picture was all of the White people that would be here, and that got me even more scared . . . I've always been a little scared of White people . . . But when I got here over the summer there were so little girls here and we spent so much time together, that we all became friends right away. (Marina, Hispanic Female, 21)

That summer program gave me a base on campus. A base from where I could build friendships and contacts. All of my girls now are the same ones I met then. We became our own clique, so even though this school is mostly white and we didn't really fit in, we always had each other, so at least we felt connected in that way. (Maya, Biracial Female, 21)

In these three excerpts the value of the sense of community created by these programs is clearly evident. This sense of belongingness engenders feelings of familiarity and belongingness between the resilient students and their academic environments. Given the historic socio-political separation between poor students of color and higher learning, as well as the cultural discontinuity discussed throughout this text, this connection is especially valuable. The result is a certain comfort and rapport built between the students and the collegiate environment, which in turn results in higher levels of social integration with the campus environment.

Two major stressors that the bridge programs directly ameliorated were *Isolation in the Collegiate Environment* (identified by 82% of students), and the *Need to be Bi-cultural* (80%). These were both addressed through the creation of not simply any sense of community, but a sense of community that was both sanctioned and encouraged by the collegiate environment. As a result, the students were provided with the rare opportunity to be both themselves and full participants in the academic culture.

In large part due to all of the students attending predominantly White higher education institutions, the students in this study expressed a great deal of anxiety around feelings of isolation within the academic environment. Additionally, their attendance at these institutions intensified their need to indeed live and flourish within two and sometimes three distinct cultures. Culture one being their home/community culture tied directly to their ethnicities and socio-economic statuses, number two being the White culture manifested by the majority of White students present, and culture three being the academic/intellectual culture valued in institutions of higher education. While many students viewed the latter two as essentially the same, others did make the distinction. Regardless, the consistent need to switch roles and personalities, as well as the accompanying changes to speech patterns (code switching), values, and habits, often created a dizzying sense of anxiety and fatigue.

To varying degrees, the students were not only cognizant of their differences—racial, ethnic, and socio-economic—but carried with them a constant sense that those difference made them trespassers on the college campus, rather than true members. The honesty with which the students shared intense feelings of isolation and insecurity about their presence on the college campuses was both extraordinary and unsettling. However, the sense of community created by membership in the special programs for economically disadvantaged students proved to be an oasis where their presence was comfortingly unremarkable. Students consistently expressed the notion of "home" and/or "taking a break" when describing their perceptions of both the conceptual community created by program membership, as well as the literal offices and spaces used by the programs:

> HEOP is a place to exhale, to get a break . . . to be yourself and not have to worry about trying to fit in. When I come here I can feel the stress leave me, it's like coming home after being away for a long time. (Marie, Haitian American Female, 20)

> Sometimes I get nervous just walking around this place (the college campus), like everyone is looking at me thinking "What is she doing here? Probably affirmative action." I don't feel that tingly feeling in my stomach when I come to EOF, or like one of our workshops or something, it's like then I'm just Natalie. (Natalie, African American Female, 23)

While program participation did not eliminate the isolation and cultural anxiety experienced by the students, it did mitigate them to the degree that the students could build up the necessary comfort level and confidence to stay in college and ultimately succeed.

In discussing the relationships between and among protective factors it should be pointed out that many factors set the foundation so that other factors can be built. For example, in this case program participation and the accompanying emotional comfort allowed the students to manufacture key dispositional factors such as *high self-esteem, bicultural selves, affability, optimism* and *help seeking tendencies*, and provided them convenient access to key environmental protective factors such as *caring college personnel, tutoring services,* and *college clubs and organizations.* In this sense, the *state/ federally funded college bridge programs* served as both a protective factor and a direct conduit to other key factors.

While the value of *caring college personnel* has been explored in this chapter, particularly in terms of informal mentoring, advising and counseling, the most commonly cited environmental protective factor was *caring school personnel from the students' k-12 experiences* (90%). In looking at the influential teachers identified by the students, while they are diverse in terms of ethnicity and gender, in comparison to the general teaching population they are disproportionately male and minority. There was no clear theme from the data that convincingly explained why this was. When students talked about their influential teachers and why they were influential, they usually omitted the teachers' ethnicity and gender and talked about what the teachers did that made them influential. Very often the only way the researcher knew the teachers' demographic background data was by asking explicitly. From the students perspective it was what the teachers were able to do which made the difference, rather than their gender or ethnicity. However, this does not mean that these characteristics were irrelevant. On the contrary, it appears that teachers who were male and/or ethnic-racial minorities were more able to influence the students in the three ways discussed below. So while being a male teacher of color in and of itself was not noteworthy to the students, being male and of color appeared to facilitate their being effective.

Three common descriptive themes emerged when students spoke of influential school personnel (teachers) from their pre-college educational lives:

1. The teachers made the students feel special.
2. The teachers were remembered as being particularly rigorous and demanding.
3. The teachers were significant beyond the classroom, that is they made themselves available before and after school, and they played important roles in extra-curricular activities.

In describing their influential teachers, in addition to phrases peppered with the usual adjectives such as "nice," "fun," and "caring," a unique recurring theme was that 91% of those who identified k-12 caring school personnel as major protective factors described how their most influential teachers made them feel academically special, and unique in positive ways. The students constantly talked of feeling uplifted and separated from their peers in a positive sense. As if they had special talents and abilities within them. These were talents and abilities that the students interpreted as having made them feel exceptional.

Perhaps surprisingly, another common descriptor was that these were the "hard" teachers, the ones who were sticklers for detail and who had high expectations for students. Thirty eight of the forty five (84%) of the students who identified teachers as protective factors characterized their influential teachers with words like "hard," "strict," "no nonsense," and "rigorous." This contradicts the stereotype of the "cool," laidback inner-city teacher who gets the kids to like them by being their friends. In describing the value of these teachers, students continuously referred to the true sense of accomplishment they got when they did receive a legitimate compliment, or when they did do well on an assignment. It was as if that teacher's comments held more weight because the students knew that whatever they had achieved, they had really earned. This is closely related to the first common description, that of making students feel academically special, in that the teachers' propensity to instill feelings of distinctiveness and uniqueness was enhanced due to the high intellectual and academic bar set in the class. The respect and gravitas earned by the teachers amplified their comments and intensified their ability to make the students feel special and uniquely talented.

The third common descriptor was that an unusually high percentage (80%) of teachers identified as influential played significant roles to the students outside of the classroom. That is, they made themselves available before and after school, and they served as faculty representatives for various extra-curricular activities, such as clubs, organizations, athletics, and community outreach initiatives. It was as if by being more than just a classroom presence, the students were able to view these teachers as three dimensional beings, with more to offer then simply school related knowledge. This helped the teachers influence the students on a level that went beyond the traditional classroom teacher/student relationship. In essence it made the teachers human.

In looking at the three criteria cited above, a certain pattern arises. Each of these teachers in their own way elevated the students' self-perceptions to a place where the students felt justified that they had the right to a life different from that of their peers.

This is especially relevant for resilient students from low SES backgrounds in that the recurring theme of their lives is often deviation from the norm of the usual trajectories of their peers. As a result, the inculcation of a sense of uniqueness is especially important. Additionally, the fact that the teachers were often academically rigorous helped suggest to these students the notion that schooling would be the appropriate path for them to move into their distinctive futures.

In speaking with students about where and how they were able to develop the high level of self-esteem discussed earlier that they found so invaluable, they often referred back to the teacher recognition explored above. Again, the academic nature of the esteem is relevant as well. Because their esteem often had its genesis in the comments of, and relationships with, teachers, as opposed to other individuals, they were able to confidently engage in academic tasks.

The rigorous nature of most of the teachers cited as influential speaks to several key protective factors and psychological stressors. In speaking of the influences of their important teachers, major protective factors such as *High Intelligence (76%), A Strong Work Ethic* (90%), *Internal Locus of Control* (92%) and *Intellectual Curiosity (52%),* were mentioned both directly and indirectly. Students spoke of how these teachers helped to instill in them a sense that they were indeed *intelligent* by raising the intellectual bar and helping the students to meet those standards. The results often meant a confirmation that they were indeed "smart." Interestingly, the road to this achievement was the exceptional amount of work required. Students spoke of the increased sense of pride in their own effort output they experienced when they excelled in these teachers' classes. It was not the "A" or "B+" per se that engendered this sense of pride in effort, but rather the course and teacher from which the high grade was achieved. This was where the level of locus of control became extant. Students began to believe in themselves when they were able to correlate the hard work with grades of which they were especially proud.

To a lesser extent, students spoke of the intellectual curiosity that their rigorous teachers engendered. Though most students who identified intellectual curiosity as a key found that curiosity as a result of an especially intriguing college course or professor, several students (38% of the 52% of total students citing intellectual curiosity as a key factor) did see the genesis of their curiosity in their high school experiences with a particularly challenging teacher.

The following excerpts capture the processes by which the students' experiences with these teachers helped to facilitate the protective factors cited above:

To this day I keep an index card that has my grade on it from my junior year English research paper, it's pinned to the bulletin board above my desk in my dorm, . . . It was the first I time I really wrote a true research paper, you know with footnotes, citations and all that stuff; I put more work into that paper than all my other high school classes combined! It was a paper on Native Son, which was like the first book I ever really enjoyed, where I was arguing that Bigger Thomas was really a hero because he lived out the fantasies of all Black people . . . anyway, I knew I had to do good job because Ms. Gordon expected a lot from us. I kept on doing extra drafts and stuff, I was so proud of that paper . . . Ms.

Gordon used to give everyone their grades on an index card, on one side would be the letter, on the back would be the comments. . . . So all that work paid off, I got a big blue A written on the card, and on the back she wrote that I actually convinced her that Bigger was a hero! Anytime I feel overwhelmed here, like maybe I don't belong, I just look at that card and feel like I can do it. (Sandra, Biracial Female, 21)

Ms. Vasquez was the one who made me want to be a Spanish teacher. She showed me that to study Spanish was more than to study a language, it is the whole Latino culture. . . . Me and all my friends took as much Spanish as possible in high school because we all spoke Spanish at home, so they were usually easy As . . . But then senior year I got Ms. Vasquez and it was a whole new ball game. She new why we took Spanish, so instead of simple grammar and stuff, she redid the curriculum. She had us reading Cervantes, García Márquez, and this women Ana Maria Matute, stuff I never hears of . . . I mean I spoke Spanish at home, but it was really more a "Spanglish" (an informal combination of Spanish and English spoken predominantly by second generation Hispanic Immigrants), so trying to understand metaphors and literary symbolism in Spanish was tough, but I learned more from her than any other teacher . . . She also made us feel good about being Latina and speaking Spanish. I never really knew there were great authors who wrote in Spanish. I never learned about that until her. . . . It helped me feel like my people were smart, not just maids and landscapers like in the movies. (Louisa, Hispanic Female, 21)

In additional to addressing the major stressor *Feelings of Low Self-Esteem* (54%) as discussed above, the rigor characterizing these teachers also addressed two more common and more pernicious stressors, *Academic Competitiveness* (74%) at the collegiate level, and *Sub-Par Pre-College Preparation* (88%).

Generally speaking, these students are the products of school systems in low socioeconomic, urban, and minority districts. As a result, their quality of education as determined by traditional barometers such as test scores, available resources, drop out rates, and college attendance, will have been lower than that of their wealthier, White suburban peers. As a consequence, when these resilient students get to college and are competing with those peers, they are at a distinct disadvantage, having to constantly play "academic catch up." This is where academic competitiveness becomes a distinct stressor. The resilient students want to prove their intellectual and academic merit, but must overcome their sub-par pre-college preparation. A major source of strength they then called upon were their experiences with the teachers cited above. They drew strength from the knowledge that they have worked hard, experienced academic success, and excelled in an intensely academic environment, even if it was just one or two classes. Often students used this knowledge to take the steps necessary to overcome these potentially destructive stressors related to college competition. Antonio's story below is an exceptionally clear demonstration of this process:

> One of my EOP counselors had this sign above his desk that said "action conquers fear." And that really struck me, cause' when I got to college I felt like I didn't really belong . . . but I knew I had to do something if I was going to make it. So my counselor asked me: "What was the hardest class you took in high school?" So I talked about my Algebra II class, and I remembered how hard I worked, and that by the end of the class the teacher was asking me to explain these concepts to the other kids in class . . . so I knew I was smart. So I started to do action, to hit the books hard and prove myself again. I knew I had at least some kind of track record of success. (Antonio, African American Male, 20)

In addition to finding strength in his past success, Antonio also reveals his fear that he may not really belong in college, that there is something fraudulent about his presence there. The sense of feeling like a "fraud" was a very common theme among these resilient students, especially when they first arrived on college campuses. They often used words and phrases such as "I didn't belong," "I slipped in through the back door," "They're going find out they made mistake and kick me out" and "I'm just not ready for this, this isn't me." However, eventually they were able to overcome these legitimacy concerns and integrate academically, and often it was the rigor of certain aspects of their high school experiences that provided the impetus.

The Value of Intellectual Curiosity and Self-Motivation

The dispositional protective factors *Intellectual Curiosity* (52%) *and Self-motivation* (86%) have proven particularly relevant to resilient students given that at many points in their lives they have found themselves swimming "against the current." Because these students are, by definition, in many ways anomalies, a recurring theme in their lives is that of being different, unique, the exception, rather than the rule. Their incongruity with respect to their environments manifests itself in a variety of ways and at a various levels.

The students often spoke in generalities, about vague amorphous feelings of difference, uniqueness and isolation. Lawrence's reflection on his freshmen orientation experience provides an example of these emotions:

> I feel like I am always the *only one*. I'll be in a situation, like on line at financial aid, and look around and think for a minute, I'm the only black guy here, its like I forget sometimes, then when I stop to think, there it is. . . . I remember during

orientation, before I had any friends, and it was lunch time in the cafeteria. I looked around and it seemed like everyone knew each other, everyone was comfortable and at ease, and I was like, how do all these people know each other, we just got here! So I was holding my tray, looking like a retard, trying to find somewhere to sit, and right away I thought if there was a Black table, I could go there. But, at that point, there was no Black table; I guess there weren't enough of us. I couldn't even find a Spanish table (Hispanic students). . . . So there I was, the *only one*. (Lawrence, African American Male, 19)

While Lawrence is primarily talking about feelings of social isolation and anxiety, the impact and significance of isolation and difference on the students' academic lives is closely related.

Unlike majority students from well educated households and communities, these resilient students could not count on being swept up in the academic current of their peers when approaching their academic tasks. Their doing well in school required more deliberate action, not only to avoid the academic lethargy characteristic of many low socioeconomic academic environments, but to focus enough to actually excel while so many peers were content with failure of mediocrity. Thus the dispositional protective factors *self-motivation* and *intellectual curiosity* often served as the fuel necessary to drive in the opposite direction of the traffic.

Intellectual curiosity was operationally defined as considerable interest in academic material for its own sake, regardless of its relationship to grades. This intellectual curiosity was highly valuable because it drove these students to engage in activities that "good" students engage in: reading, asking questions, debating ideas, attending lectures, etc. even when their peer groups may have shown little or no interest in such activities. When learning about ideas became something the resilient students chose to do simply because it sparked their own interest and "felt good," they were less reliant on academic peer pressure to do well, which was often absent from their lives. As discussed earlier, while some students got their intellectual interest peaked during high school, for the majority it was college.

Deborah's "light bulb story" below speaks to the power of intellectual curiosity:

I remember being in a women's history class and we had to read this book called "The Feminine Mystique." My professor, it was like she had this way of explaining that was like so real . . . And that was it, it was like a light bulb going off . . . I went to the library and read everything I could on women's liberation and gender studies and stuff. It became my thing . . . I remember once I was reading a one of the text books from that class, in my dorm room but it was that semester was over, my friend was like "What class is that for?" And I was like, it's not for any

class, I'm just reading it. She looked at me like I was crazy. But I didn't care, I
enjoyed that stuff so much, I made it my major. (Deborah, Bi-Racial Female, 22)

Not only did this sort of intellectual curiosity help the participants become "better" students, but it also helped them become academically inte-
grated into their college environments, which is an historical correlate to
college success.

It should be pointed out that true intellectual curiosity is rare in any demographic group, particularly traditionally aged college students, 18–21
years old. Thus, while it appears that most wealthy White students also lack
intellectual curiosity at that stage, the difference is that often they can excel
anyway due to both their cultural capital, and the engrained academic expectations with which they and their peers were raised. Generally speaking,
potentially resilient students do not possess these assets to the same degree,
thus their intellectual curiosity takes on even more meaning and importance.

Even for students who have demonstrated academic resilience, intellectual
curiosity was not overly common. As a result, for those students who were
not able to utilize that curiosity as a tool to fight the current, and move in a
different direction, self-motivation was the primary means.

Self-motivation was determined to exist when students both talked about
themselves as being self-motivated, and when they described situations where
they relied primarily on themselves to take action related to enhancing their
educational achievement. Examples of common actions include forcing oneself to stay home and study when friends wanted to go out; seeking out internship, job and tutoring opportunities, and scholarships; working long hours for
low wages to pay for school related expenses; and doing homework throughout high school, without parents having to remind them. While it may seem
obvious, it bares stating that self-motivation does not occur in a vacuum. For
the most part, in order for self-motivation to be in effect, the students must
have received the prerequisite affective and psychological nourishment from
significant others in their lives. As discussed above, this was often in the form
of loving mothers, caring teachers, and empathetic counselors. Furthermore,
as is made clear by the preceding examples, in order for self-motivation to be
effective, their must be environmental resources with which the student can
interact. High school and college support and tutoring programs funded by
local, state, and federal agencies often provided these students with resources
with which they could interact. Without such resources, the self-motivation
these students describe is often impotent.

Self-motivation is not equivalent to complete independence. Self-motivation is a dispositional protective factor that requires the availability of environmental and familial resources in order for it to be meaningful.

Exactly how these students manifested their sense of self-motivation and used it to excel academically varied a great deal from student to student. However, a common theme that arose was the growing sense of self-efficacy and environmental mastery discussed throughout this chapter. This evolving sense of self-efficacy provided these students with the track record and confidence to actively seek out their academic goals. The following excerpts are students discussing events in their life when they felt they exhibited self-motivation, and how past accomplishments helped fuel them:

> Because it was a community college when I first got here I treated it like it was what we called "the 13th grade," like just an extension of high school . . . when I got my first paper back in Comp. 1, I was blinded by so much red. The professor tore it to shreds with red comments everywhere. I was embarrassed and scared. I thought maybe I didn't belong in college. . . . If I was getting a grade like this in a community college, imagine when I transferred to a four year. . . . I went back to my dorm and actually cried. Then I got an email from my high school English teacher asking how I was doing. When I told her about the paper, she talked me through it, reminded me of how I struggled in her class at first and then went on to be one of her best students. . . . The next day I went to my professor's office hours, went over the paper with her, rewrote it, and then had my roommate read it over, then went to the writing center to have a tutor go over it, and I made even more changes, I was determined to do better. . . . Not only did I end up with a B+ on that paper, the professor and I became close and she ended up writing me a letter of recommendation when I transferred to State college (pseudonym for the 4 year school she currently attends). What I learned from that incident was that you can't just give up. I have had obstacles, but I can get over if I just keep pushing. And while other people have to help, in the end it's just up to me. (Wendy, Bi-racial Female, 22)

In addition to drawing on her past accomplishments to provide her with confidence, in Wendy's case we see the process of several other protective factors becoming enacted as a result of her self-motivation. As discussed above, self-motivation alone has little impact. For Sonia, her caring teachers and the institutional services facilitated the efficacy of her self-motivation.

For most of the students in this study, the process of talking about their educational achievement was novel. For the most part, they never had reason to analyze their educational actions and pinpoint how and why they were doing what they were.

As a result, initially other students were less aware of the interdependence with which they achieved their goals, but as they described their accomplishments they became increasingly cognizant of how other people were integral parts of their success. Lamar's realizations below capture much of how this phenomenon often transpired:

> My father always told me "you come into this world alone and you leave alone." And that always stayed with me. I know that I am the only one responsible for me. In high school I always prided myself on not having to ask anyone for any help. Who else can I count on? But now I don't really know, because I am who I am because of other people. And without others what would I do? I am pretty smart in most subjects, but when it comes to math, I just get frustrated. In high school I was able to get by, but here I was struggle with Intermediate Algebra. I was spending 80% of my study time on that one class, and still pulling C-s and Ds. . . . Before the midterm I saw a little flyer announcing what they called a supplemental instruction group, it's like a study group, but led by a tutor who sits in on the class. And at first I didn't want to go, cause' I thought "I have to do this myself." But obviously that wasn't working. I got myself to go and it really helped a lot. I saw other people struggling like me and that made me feel better. (Lamar, African American Male, 20)

Like many of the students Lamar was so attached to the notion that complete independence was the most important goal, that he was reticent to use his self-motivation to engage others into his cause. However, fortunately for his academic status, he was able to reconcile his belief in autonomy with an evolving understanding of interdependence. And while this phenomenon has much to do with the emotional maturity levels of the students given their ages, it does appear that an understanding of the interdependence necessary for achievement is crucial for most of these students.

Bicultural Selves

The value and need to be adept at being bicultural (88%) has proven such an integral dispositional protective factor, and has crossover significance to so many familial and environmental factors that to couple it with only one or two other factors would not only be an artificial contrivance, but would also do a disservice to its magnitude. It may be surprising that while it has been cited as an essential protective factor by so many students, the "need to be bi-cultural" has also been cited as a major psychological stressor (80%).

To be bicultural refers to the acquired skills associated with effectively operating in various environments, particularly the student's home/ethnic/ racial environment, and that of the academic world. The consequence for not handling these roles effectively can be social marginalization and/or academic failure. What should be added briefly here is the reality that the flip side of the stress induced by biculturalism is its value as a tool used to effectively negotiate the formal academic environment, an environment which is to varying degrees antithetical to the students' "home cultures."

Being bicultural extended deeply into many of the key protective factors discussed here, and is explored within the context of those sections. When students acquiesced to their readiness to class jump, when they sought out help from the culturally different, and when they commuted to non-neighborhood schools, they were exhibiting their "bi-cultural" adeptness. Throughout each of these situations they had to adapt to new and distinct cultures while maintaining ties to their origins.

Because Step 3 covers a multitude of protective factors working in context and concert it is the most comprehensive and lengthy part of the Resilience Cycle. However, without Spoke Four where the student recognizes and refines these protective factors, it is unlikely that these students would have been able to overcome the significant obstacles they have, and succeeded as much as they have.

Chapter Seven

The Cycle in Context:
Spoke 4 "Evaluating and Enhancing"

Spoke 4, *The student recognizes the effectiveness of the protective factors and continues to refine and implement them,* reminds us that like life, the resilience process continues to be an unfolding and evolving process for these students. This is especially true for these students because they are in the midst of their achievement, and while they are all doing well, they are not yet finished with their academic journeys.

As with most activities engaged in repeatedly, these students have grown increasingly adept at utilizing and implementing their protective factors. This conscious awareness that while the protective factors are working, they can and should be modified is the essence of Spoke 4.

APPRECIATING WHAT WORKS: STUDENTS SPEAK

Before these students could modify effective protective factors, they had to recognize and appreciate their efficacy. This appreciation process took several different forms, but most often occurred when some concrete validation of their efforts was presented to them (e.g. earning an unexpectedly high grade, making the dean's list, being awarded a lucrative scholarship, gaining admission to a competitive school/program, etc.). It was as if once they received this clear evidence of their success, they then asked themselves how? They then were able to recognize the value of whatever the answer was.

Below are several examples of students coming to these realizations as a result of their various rewards:

> I am a business major, so English and writing and stuff was never my strong area, but obviously I couldn't avoid it, I mean English and writing classes are

required, especially your first year . . . what added to the pressure was that I had to keep my GPA above a 3.25 or I could lose my scholarship, so it wasn't just about trying to do as good as I can, it was about money . . . somehow I get through the first semester freshmen comp. class with a B, but second semester I had a much harder teacher, she was serious, much more demanding than the last guy, so I knew I was in trouble . . . after I got a C− on the first paper I was really scared. This guy on my floor then told me about how he always goes to the campus writing center and has never gotten below an A- on any paper he took there. So I figured I would try . . . I found some good tutors there, and on my next paper I got a B+. After that I was sold. I went there with every paper for that class and ended up with an A− in it. (Antonio, African American Male, 23)

One of the things I started to realize was that teachers could be your friend or your enemy depending, so why not make them your friends as much as possible . . . At the start of my junior year at St. Mary's (Tina's high school) I knew that I wanted to try for one of the ten $1,000 PTA scholarships that the school gives out. It was partially for the money, but more for like the recognition, you know to feel special. But I saw the application and you needed two teacher recom- mendations and at least one administrator. So I decided that this year I was really going to buddy up to them. Like ask a lot of questions, stay after to help, get involved with extracurricular stuff all that . . . I ended up having plenty of people to choose from and winning one of the scholarships. That really made it clear to me that teachers and stuff, they not only can be a huge help, but they kind of want to help. I carried that idea with me to college and it's worked out really good so far. (Tina, Bi-racial Female, 22)

When I got that acceptance letter to grad school, I felt like this huge relief come over me. But more than that, it all came into focus. Like I knew, really knew for the first time that all those hours in the library definitely were worth it. All those missed parties, and early morning, they definitely did the trick. Knowing that is real important. When I get to grad school I will be able to do it again, and it will be easier, because now I am not hoping that it pays off, I know it does (Mario, Hispanic Male, 23)

What is evident through these representative vignettes is that at certain points these students clearly recognized the value of specific protective factors, and once that recognition took place, their desire and propensity to continue to employ them was reinforced.

Strategic Modification of Protective Factors: Students Speak

A valuable next step subsequent to appreciating what worked, and one that really was essential in helping these students excel beyond statistical expec- tations, was the modification and refinement of protective factors that then followed. These students not only knew that these resources worked, but they took the next step of modifying them to both maximize their effectiveness and to fit them into new situations.

The three examples above are continued below to show how this refinement often transpired:

> Because I went to the writing center so much, I started to get to know the tutors really well. And one thing that's strange about that place is that they have like two different kinds of tutors, like some are students and some are like older, professional tutors . . . and I found that when I meet with the older ones I usually get better grades, I think they know more and stuff. Anyway . . . but the thing is that the older ones are usually only there during the day, and you have to make a specific appointments with them, while the student ones would usually cover the night shifts when they had these open hours. So after my first year, and even now, I always make sure to make an appointment and go during the day, that way I know that I will get a good paper out of it . . . It is kind of a pain, because I do have more time in the evenings, but it is totally worth it. (Antonio, African American Male, 23)

> Since I've been here (in college) I have been even more focused on getting to know my professors as much as possible . . . I especially do it (get to know her professors) in the big lecture classes, because there it so hard to be noticed. . . . in the smaller classes it's much easier to get to know the professor, all you have to do is talk a lot, and you know, stay after a bit and get help, it's real like intimate. But I realized that in the big ones there are so many students that they (the professors) don't know me. I realize this when I needed help in my intro to psyc. course and I went to office hours, and the guy was like, "Who are you again?" That's when I realized that especially for those lecture hall type classes you have to go see the teachers early on, on a one on one basis. That's the only way you're going to get to know them so they can help you. (Tina, Bi-racial Female, 22)

> Even though I only have like one semester to go, I am more focused now than ever. My goal is to get a 3.75 this semester which I never got before, so I had to revamp, like redo, my study schedule. I realized that I was spending the same amount of time studying for classes that I was good at as I was for those that I wasn't. Like my African American history classes are pretty much easier for me, but by European histories are really tough. So what I made sure to do this semester was to spend two hours studying European for every one hour I spent on African. I know its like a little structured and stuff, but it seems to make more sense to me. (Mario, Hispanic Male, 23)

In each of these cases the students followed up their recognition of the value of the protective factors by strategically modifying and enhancing them.

Another common theme here is that these students were not changing their approaches because they weren't working; they modified them because they *were* working. This unique and highly developed strategic approach leads to the evolution of the protective factors to the point where they become even more effective than before. As mentioned earlier, this extra effort often made the difference between good and outstanding performance, and accounts for much of their academic resilience.

Emerging Confidence: Students Speak

Another important aspect of Spoke 4 is the confidence that recognition of success engenders. Though somewhat amorphous, the concept of confidence can be directly related to two key protective factors identified by 92% of these students, namely *High Self-Esteem* and *Internal Locus of Control*. Both their feeling good about themselves and their belief in their own abilities to effectuate desired outcomes were strengthened by the genuine confidence they acquired as a result concrete success. Very often this confidence was amplified when the students recognized the value of their protective factors and took control over how and when to employ them. This found confidence both made them feel good about themselves as students (high self-esteem) and bolstered their beliefs in themselves to effectively overcome any obstacles to reaching their goals (internal locus of control).

The narrative excerpts below reveals how many of these students turned appreciation of success into valuable confidence. The first set demonstrates how confidence contributed to self-esteem, and the second how it facilitates a sense of internal locus of control:

I try to have faith that if I work hard and stuff that things will work out, but the truth is that I am really skeptical and usually only believe something if I see it and what not . . . like I really only gained confidence in myself as a student when it was the end of my freshman year and I got my grades for the spring semester and realized I made dean's list. You know it was really when I looked back and saw that everything worked out that I really began to feel confident, like I do belong here, like I am a real student. (Antoinette, Haitian American Female, 20)

Confidence is something that I thought I had a lot of ever since I was young, but really I think that was kind of a fake confidence, like more like boasting. Cause I would talk a lot about how much I was gonna do and how I was going to a top college and all that, but I don't know if I really believed all of it. . . . when I actually did make it to Lincoln (University), it was like a big exhale, like I really did make it. That was when real confidence came, because I could see how things did work out. (Andrea, Hispanic Female, 19).

In both of these cases the students' achievements engendered self-esteem because they were built on tangible and concrete achievement. Thus the self-esteem was not false and hollow rhetoric or bravado, but rather built on authentic feelings of accomplishment. This is an important distinction. Youth culture, particularly music, and sports are replete with boasting and public bravado. Many youth will talk about how great they are and how good they feel about themselves, but often they do not really believe these claims because they lack legitimate support. This false bravado can be dangerous because the students feel an obligation to make improbable claims about what they can and will do, then end up feeling ashamed and disappointed because not only do these claims not come to fruition, but they knew all along that they were implausible to begin with. Very often fear of further feelings of academic incompetence push students away from new school related challenges, thus cementing their academic futures.

The importance and value of Spoke Four lies primarily with its emphasis on the student's ability to recognize what is working, what's not, and why. This recognition allows for both the refinement of key protective factors and the appreciation, and resulting confidence, of their value. Additionally, it is important to recognize that the refinement part of the process is not a one time-occurrence. It was done continuously as new challenges presented themselves. This a major feature of Step Five.

Chapter Eight

The Cycle in Context: Spoke 5 "Developed Habits and Goals"

SPOKE 5: THE CONSTANT AND CONTINUOUS REFINEMENT AND IMPLEMENTATION OF PROTECTIVE FACTORS, ALONG WITH THE EVOLVING VISION OF THE STUDENT'S DESIRED DESTINATION, SUSTAIN THE STUDENT'S PROGRESS.

Spokes 3 and 4 clearly articulate the value of the various protective factors and protective factor combinations, as well as the importance of continuous modification. Additionally, the confidence engendered raises academic self-esteem and the students' belief in themselves to handle forthcoming challenges. By means of extension, Spoke 5 emphasizes both this enduring aspect of proven protective factors and their ability to sustain the students as they move closer to the goals that they envision for themselves.

RESOURCES BECOME ROUTINE: STUDENTS' SPEAK

As alluded to earlier, the value of the protective factors are not that they worked once and then were discarded. Their power really came when they were transformed from isolated strategies and resources to habitual behaviors.

The most common form of sustained and habituated environmental protective factors came in how the students continuously took advantage of both *Caring K–12 School Personnel* (90%) and *College Personnel* (72%). Taking advantage of these resources was predicated on a very common dispositional protective factor, namely the students' tendencies and willingness to quickly seek help from others when faced with challenges (82%).

Lucy's experiences documented below demonstrate how these resilient students began to rely on supportive people continuously as new challenges arrived:

> It's almost like a reflex with me, liking running home to mommy when there's a problem, but for me it's not my mother, it's Miss. K. (Lucy's guidance counselor, Ms. Kazinsky) . . . like when I was picking my classes, you know for the first semester here (in college), and it was like there were so many choices. I mean some stuff I had to take, like English, but I had choices too. And I remember real clearly, it was like midnight and I was in my dorm room trying to register on-line and I was like freaking out. I e-mailed Miss. K. immediately and told her to call me in the morning, whenever she got the e-mail. Even though there was a college counselor I got assigned to, I wanted Miss. K. She called me at like 7 in the morning, and we talked for a good half hour she totally calmed me down and gave me good advice. . . . I apologized for always bothering her, but she didn't mind. I still go to her when I need something. . . . It's like, you know that kid in Charlie Brown, that one with the blanket, like he always needs it. That's how I feel about Miss. K. sometimes. It's kind of embarrassing, but that's the way it is (Lucy, Hispanic Female, 19)

As with many of the students who identified people as significant protective factors, Lucy built sustained connections with knowledgeable adults with whom she felt comfortable turning to over and over again. And because these mentors proved helpful consistently and in a variety of situations, the students turned to them repeatedly as various issues arose.

The degree of comfort and understanding characterizing the mentor/ protégé relationships discussed here was significant in that this rapport facilitated frequent and consistent contact. Had the students not felt so close and welcomed by the mentors, it is unlikely that they would have turned to them so frequently, and in such a variety of ways. In essence, because these students had such positive experiences and outcomes when contacting these mentors, such contact became increasingly habitual.

Another major protective factor which was habitually employed was the students' ability to motivate themselves (86%). From the students' perspectives, this wide-ranging protective factor was often actuated by related protective factors, primarily their *Desire/Willingness to "Class Jump"* (94%) and their *Sense of Obligation to Family* (94%). Manuel's narrative below is highly representative of how many of the students made self-motivation a habit through both their desire to get ahead and the sense of duty they felt toward their families:

> One of the things that I started to realize was that as much as I love my family and do what I do for them, at the end of the day it is up to me. It's about me

getting things done. Every night, well almost every night, before I go to sleep I make a list of three things I will do to the next day to help me reach my goals . . . the rule is that I can't do anything I want, like for fun, until I get the list done . . . like hard things like go to the library for three hours, write three pages of a paper or whatever, or read thirty pages of a text book, that kind of stuff. And the funny thing is that at night I'm all energized and stuff so I write down all this ambitious type of stuff, but then in the morning, I don't feel like it. And all I want to do is go hangout down the hall. Or go to the gym and play ball or whatever, but I know I can't, but no one is pushing me, like I could go play ball and who would stop me? So there I have to motivate myself to do the list first, even though I don't feel like it . . . that's what I mean when I say it's up to me. Nobody is there to push me, I have to do it, it's on my shoulders but I do it for them (Manuel's family) so that they can be proud of where I go . . . I made a promise to my mom that I would buy her a house en el campo (in the country) one day, I made her that promise because I know all that she's done for me, what she sacrificed . . . it's all tied together. I get the good grades, then I can make good money, then I can live good and get my mom that house. But at the end of the day it's up to me. It used to be much more hard to get that list done, but now I usually just do it. I get myself up and I get to work. (Manuel, Hispanic Male, 22)

The simultaneous presence of individual effort and group affiliation evident in Manuel's narrative was a common phenomenon for many of the students. While they acknowledge what their families have done for them and want to move up in social and economic class to provide for them, the day to day tasks necessary to reach these ends can be solitary work. The isolation of the academic journey is often acerbated by the fact that these students were all the first in the families to go to college. As a result, very often family members, especially parents, only had vague notions of what it really takes to excel in college. Thus while family members were able to provide support, motivation, and sources of inspiration, the students had to become highly self-motivated in order to meet their ongoing academic objectives on a daily basis.

CLARITY OF GOALS AND SUSTAINED MOTIVATION: STUDENTS SPEAK

By far the single most common motivating factor for these students was their vision of where they wanted to be as a result of their education, and what they wanted to do once they got there. Several commonly identified dispositional protective factors relate directly to this vision realization dynamic: *Desire/ willingness to "class jump"* (94%), *Sense of obligation to family* (94%), *Persistence* (94%), *Internal Locus of Control* (92%), *and* perhaps most importantly, *Strong Future Orientations* (86%). As a result of this complex psycho-social amalgam these students were able to sustain their drive, and actually increase effort as they moved closer to their goals. The following excerpt from Sharita illustrates how these factors worked interdependently, creating visions of success that propelled students toward achievement:

> I knew that I wanted to be a teacher ever since I was 8 years old. Me and my cousins used to play school in our basement and I always made sure to be the teacher. I loved telling them what to do and making little tests and things like that. It was so fun, we used to play for hours . . . when I was in high school, at the beginning of high school, I really started with thinking that it was a real job path for me. I would look at my teachers, and none of them lived in Newark. They all lived in nice suburban towns; it was like, even though the joke is that teachers don't make money, I knew they kind of did because all my teachers had money, at least compared to us. That's what I wanted for me, that little house in the suburbs with a green lawn and a doghouse and stuff, all safe and clean, so I attached teaching to that dream. . . . I remember telling my mom that I wanted to be a teacher and she was so happy, she said she would be so proud if I did that, that being a college graduate would be something for the family to be proud of, that I could be a role model and all . . . when I got here (in college) and started to get into my major, I got real discouraged for a while because it was harder that I thought. You had all these requirements, like the state test for teaching and I have to keep my GPA high, it was hard, but I know I have to keep going, because I know where I want to get to . . . Like right now I have three finals next week and they're not gonna be easy, but I have to do it. Since I got this far, I just have to keep going. Whenever I catch myself slacking, not studying hard or whatever, I always remember why I am here and what I want to be. That always helped to push me. . . . This semester coming up I am going to be doing my student teaching and I am so excited. It's like I can see myself teaching, having my own class, talking to the kids, it's right there, just like in my basement. Knowing that makes it easy to study for my finals now, I'm almost there. (Sharita, African American Female, 22)

In Sharita's narrative it is clear that she is using her desire to be a teacher, and all that means to her (e.g. financial security, pride for her family, etc.), as a motivating force to help her meet the requisite challenges along the way. As with many of the students, Sharita uses her clear sense of what she wants repeatedly and in a variety of ways.

It is important to point out here that in order for this vision to be truly powerful, it must hold profound meaning and significance for the students. If Sharita were indifferent or even ambivalent about becoming a teacher, then her vision of achieving that goal would be far less potent. It is precisely because of the importance and worth placed on the desired outcome that it maintains the far reaching influence that it does. Without this value, and the corresponding motivation, many of these students would have had a great deal of difficulty staying on track, especially given the extraordinary amount and variety of hurdles and obstacles engendered by their socioeconomic status and minority backgrounds.

It is important to point out that while Spoke 5 is theoretically the final one; in reality the process of resilience is continuous, especially as new challenges continue to arise. As goals and situations change, the students will employ and manifest appropriate protective factors. In many ways, the resilience cycle will begin over and over again in different iterations to match whatever new realities arise. Consequently, the Cycle should not be viewed as fixed structure, but rather as an organic evolving framework that is generally representative of the process of resilience for a majority of these students.

Chapter Nine

Facilitating Resilience: Practical Implications

The word "facilitating" in the chapter title above is particularly appropriate when discussing the promotion of resilience. Based on our research, professional experience, and teaching we have come to the inevitable conclusion that one person cannot make, force, compel or coerce another person to be resilient. Because resilience necessitates sustained efforts and interactions *over time,* there must be a consistent drive within the individual to continuously meet challenges as they arise. Imposition from the outside simply would not work, it would be like taking someone who has never trained, nor wanted to train, as a runner, and "making them" complete the New York City marathon within six hours. No amount of reward or punishment could ensure that person's success. However, there are myriad interventions that could support, encourage, and promote (i.e. "facilitate") those who have the desire and necessary talent to achieve more than what has been statistically portended as a result of their background. With these understandings in place, we put forth the following recommendations based on the research presented, and then create separate categories for ideas for working with individuals, and ideas for working with groups.

RECOMMENDATIONS FOR FACILITATING RESILIENCE WITH INDIVIDUALS

Attempting to facilitate resilience often requires certain changes in disposition and expectations. As discussed briefly earlier, we must open up the sense of possibility as to what is possible and by whom. Part of this change is looking at all students as truly potentially resilient, or as *resilience in waiting.* Thus the goal is not necessarily how can we give these students what they need to succeed, but rather how can we tap into these students' existing strengths and help them harness those strengths to become successful. Obviously this means that they will have to acquire new skills along the way, but this new thinking is premised on the belief that the student's base is healthy and loaded with possibility. The goal then becomes, in part, to assist the students in identifying their strength and applying it to academic tasks. The formal and informal mentors who arose to assist the resilient students in this study understood this paradigm shift and used that understanding to be effective.

The importance of these influential adults (mostly k–12 & college level educators) for the students in this study cannot be underestimated. In essence, most of these individuals served as social capital, providing these students with the insights and access to academia (and academic values) that they often lacked at home. Given this reality, we encourage those who are attempting to build valuable personal relationships with potentially resilient students to remain cognizant of the following:

Providing Cultural Capital: Low SES/ethnic minority students may particularly benefit from being mentored by educators who both possess, and are eager to share, *insider* knowledge. Whether that knowledge is academic (subject based) or procedural (how to negotiate educational organizations effectively), exposure to these resources may prove invaluable for this population. Often there is a tendency to take the presence of this type of cultural capital for granted. However, often even the most seemingly basic academic understandings may not be part of the students' experiences. For example, upon entering college many of the students in this study did not know what a grade point average was, nor how it was calculated; had never created a bibliography nor completed a science lab; did not know what types of subjects fell into the "liberal arts" category; and had only a very vague idea of what graduate school was, and why one might attend. Consequently, as part of their interaction with these students, educators/ counselors may have to take affirmative and intentional steps to provide this type of background information rather than assume its presence.

Sanctioning Students: In counseling and guiding these students, educators should be aware of their power to legitimize and sanction student goals and aspirations through positive encouragement and support. Again, the issue of taking certain realities for granted is evident. Educators must not take for granted that these students posses *genuine* confidence in their abilities to overcome obstacles and achieve in academic and professional realms. As explored earlier, these students often receive a massive number of both overt and subtle messages that question their academic competence. Furthermore, even when students are boastful or confident on the outside, these expressions often belie serious amounts of academic insecurity and doubt. Relatively simple words of encouragement from educators whom the students view as accomplished and knowledgeable can go a long way toward building invaluable internal loci of control. When these respected mentors articulate their sincere belief in their protégés, the sincerity of the student's own belief in her or himself becomes more pronounced.

Engendering Persistence and Locus of Control: Those interested in promoting resilience in individuals should incorporate the fact that two dispositional protective factors utilized repeatedly throughout the students' mitigation of risk were *Persistence* and *Internal Locus of Control*. These closely related attributes are intimately linked to the students' ability to build on previous success. Students are willing to continuously expend effort *(persistence)* only if they believe that their efforts will be rewarded *(internal locus of control)*. However, what tends to generate these two valuable dynamics is the individual student's belief in him or herself, specifically in his or her belief in their academic abilities. Consequently, it is not surprising that *High Academic Self-esteem* was identified as essential for academic success by ninety four percent of the students in the study. What is surprising however is that while high academic self-esteem was overwhelmingly cited as valuable, feelings of *Low Academic Self-esteem* were cited as a major *risk* factor by fifty four percent of the students. This apparent contradiction may be evidence of the ambivalent and vicissitudinary nature of the students' beliefs in themselves and their academic abilities. What is certain however, is that potentially resilient students need to build their academic self-esteem and confidence based on *authentic* achievement, not shallow and hollow praise.

One reality that makes it difficult to build academic self-esteem in students is that it can be a laborious and time consuming process. The students in this study developed their belief and confidence over time, as they reflected on previous struggles and achievements. Once they were able to see the connections between effort and achievement, they began to believe more in themselves.

The other relevant issue here is that the more arduous the achievement task, the stronger and more valuable the self-esteem gleaned. Well meaning educators often provide shallow and empty praise, and most often the students realize this. After a while the hollow praise ceases to enhance self-esteem, and can actually begin to make the student question her/his ability.

Educators committed to promoting academic resilience and esteem should encourage students to reflect on specific instances when extensive effort (studying, research, etc.) resulted in a positive academic outcome. This type of reflection can motivate students authentically, because it is based on specific realities, rather than broad, fictitious generalities. Additionally, if a student does not have an appropriate academic experience on which to draw, he or she can focus on a non-academic incident where effort was rewarded. Either way, the goal is to enhance the students' beliefs in themselves by demonstrating instances where efforts were clearly rewarded. This type of authentic self-esteem can serve as a base from which many of he other valuable protective factors can be launched.

Making it "Okay" to Achieve: Related to the notion that educators can legitimize the potentially resilient students' academic aspirations is that often it is necessary to convince these students that to excel academically and professionally is not necessarily a betrayal of their racial and academic backgrounds. As has been explored previously in the text, this issue was often especially prevalent for the male students. As a result educators may have to provide evidence that academic achievement is indeed "okay." This can be done by presenting examples of high achieving individuals who are not perceived as "sell-outs," and by convincing the students that often the most effective way to change the system is to gain prominence within it.

Recasting Risk as Asset: A general strategy for effectively working with potentially resilient students is to figure out ways of turning their apparent disadvantages into possible advantages. For example many of the Hispanic students had to overcome language barriers during their early academic lives because Spanish rather than English was their first language. However, upon mastering English and excelling in academics, they now have the advantage of being bilingual. By pointing out how this skill makes them more valuable in the work world, the student is then rewarded for what had been a barrier.

Other specific examples of this include students who were hired to work as RAs (Resident Advisors) or orientation counselors in part because they appeared to understand the needs of students from similar backgrounds who may be struggling to connect and thrive on the college campus. Similar to the language example above, having overcome a potential barrier (in this case a marginalized/urban/low SES background) these students are then more valuable as sources of information and understanding for others.

Those working with potentially resilient students should search for ways to help the students mine their hard earned achievements for valuable skills, attributes, and knowledge that can then be transformed into professional and academic success.

Additionally, for those students who were relatively new immigrants, instead of looking at their immigrant statuses as problems that need to be fixed, mentors may effectively build on that status, turning it into a strength. By acknowledging the courage, will, and effort that often characterize the immigration experience, mentors can help these students feel pride, and use that pride as a motivating force.

One caveat here is that as with any research conclusions about particular sub-populations, we must be careful not to turn them into stereotypical assumptions. While a primary purpose of qualitative research, such as that which has been conducted in the present study, is to identify emerging themes common to the student research participants as a whole, we must not forget that these students had more differences from each other than shared characteristics. Consequently, while they may have shared socioeconomic and educational and background criteria, they are all complex, multifaceted individuals, taking their own unique paths toward their unlikely academic success. As such, the above conclusions should be seen as a guide of what *may* be valid/helpful, rather than a step by step instruction booklet that applies equally to all.

IDEAS AND SUGGESTION FOR WORKING WITH GROUPS

Based on the research conducted here on individual students, as well as our professional experiences in a variety of educational and clinical settings, we have come to certain conclusions as to how resilience can be facilitated at the macro level. However, these suggestions are made with the understanding that within these larger contexts the core work of resilience facilitation will still take place on the individual/interpersonal level. As such, the ideas explored below are intended to create environments that enhance the likelihood and propensity for academic success.

Provide and Utilize Multiple and Diverse Protective Resources: The extent and pervasiveness of the risk faced by the students in this study cannot be overstated. Evidence of its scale and enormity can be found in the fact that for each risk factor documented *multiple* (usually three to five) major protective factors had to work in unison in order to produce successful results. Unlike in movies and popular media, one good teacher, one strong parent, or one scholarship opportunity alone was never really enough. As a result, those interested in promoting resilience so that more poor and minority students can go to college must be committed to providing an *array* of protective factor resources that address multiple types of needs.

Understanding this reality, it becomes clear why the state and federal college bridge/opportunity programs were so important and successful for these students. These programs are designed explicitly to increase the numbers of economically and educationally disadvantaged students who enroll and graduate from college. What makes them both unique, and effective, is that they provide a wide range of multiple services designed to counteract the students' acute levels of disadvantage and risk. While specific details differ from program to program, most offer substantial financial aid, free tutoring, comprehensive emotional and academic counseling, summer remedial programs, cultural enrichment, and personal development opportunities. This broad array of services serves as a metaphorical shield, combing with the students' motivation and work ethic to produce success.

While not every situation will allow for such expensive and comprehensive services, whenever possible, those in charge of facilitating resilience should maximize the amount and types of resources available.

Create and Provide Structure, Rigor, and High Expectations to Enhance Persistence, Strong Work Ethic, and Internal Locus of Control: When the students in this study described what made their valuable schools and teachers effective they very often emphasized the high expectations, structure and rigor that characterized those learning environments. The students also expressed their impressions that to a certain extent there was a causal relationship between primary dispositional protective factors (i.e. persistence, strong work ethic, and the development and value of regimented study plans) and this structure and rigor.

The educational literature on teacher attitudes toward low SES and minority children are replete with findings of their exhibiting low expectations and pity for these students. Those responsible for creating and monitoring educational initiatives designed to promote resilience should guard against this tendency and remind educators of the disempowerment that these attitudes engender. This may be much easier said than done. Given the egregious academic deficits that are sometimes exhibited by these students it is easy to understand why teachers may want to lower the bar in attempts to build self-esteem. Good intentions aside we must avoid this approach. As was exhibited by the students in this study, the only achievements which provided enduring lifts to self-esteem were those that were based on hard work, persistence, and real achievement. Not only do students eventually become aware of hollow achievement, but such achievements can give students false senses of academic readiness, which can then lead to profound frustrations and disappointment.

Interestingly, despite the fact that the students in the study believed that many of their teachers did hold high expectations for them, enough of their teachers didn't that a vast majority of the students found themselves playing academic catch up when they got to college. Consequently, not only are high expectations invaluable, but helping students acquire a willingness to persist and enhancing their internal loci of control, are essential. These were the primary dispositional attributes they used to get themselves to do what was necessary to overcome the gap between their preparedness and the academic expectations of their collegiate environments.

The most effective way to increase internal locus of control and persistence is to help students reflect on and identify times and experiences when not giving up and taking action produced desirable results. This can be tricky. On one hand we are saying demand high expectations, and on the other we are saying have students reflect on success. How do we facilitate both success and challenge? While different situations call for different specifics, the general equation should be that increases in challenge should be accompanied by increases in scaffolding and support. It is unfair to demand that students meet high expectations without providing them the assistance they need to do so.

An illustrative example of how this dynamic plays itself out can be gleaned by taking a look at one of the state funded college bridge programs that so many of the students found essential to their academic success.

The goal of this particular program was to admit economically and academically disadvantaged students, most of whom would not have met the academic requirements for admission if not for the program, and both retain and graduate those students by having them meet same academic criteria as the university's general population.

By virtually any standard these are ambitious goals, requiring students to meet relatively high expectations. Consequently, the program must provide enough support to warrant such ambition. The scaffolding in this case includes the following: An intensive six week residential summer program where students are introduced to college level coursework, provided emotional counseling, matched with mentors, introduced to other students, and given an overall preview of the campus and college life; financial aid and support covering virtually all expenses; monitors to keep track of their academic progress, and to intercede when students get off track; professional and student tutors for major subjects; ongoing field trips to experience cultural events; and their own computer lab. Yes, these resources are both extensive and expensive, but they are necessary given the intense and wide-ranging risk factors that these students had to overcome. As these students successfully moved through the program and their college educations, they were able to reflect on their success and draw strength from it. However, without the comprehensive and effectual support, it is unlikely that achievement would have followed.

Perhaps the biggest cause of failure of academic programs designed to facilitate the academic success of "at-risk" students is that they underestimate the breadth and depth of the challenges at hand. These initiatives must recognize the length of the journeys they are attempting to facilitate, and provide the support necessary to keep the goals within the realm of practicality. Then they will have produced enough true successes to feed the student's sense of academic self-esteem, and in turn to promote the necessary levels of persistence and internal locus of control.

Encourage Exposure to High Achieving Students

Throughout the text there was much discussion, bother directly and indirectly, about the influence of peer group norms and trends on these resilient students. And while it was true that for the most part these students were able to resist or eschew the waves of academic resignation and failure characteristic of many of their community peers, this challenging endeavor was exceedingly difficult. So much so that it makes one wonder how many other bright, hard-working, intellectually curious poor youth would have reached their academic goals had they not been derailed by the ubiquitous, and understandable desire to "fit in."

Programs designed to facilitate resilience should strive to give low socio-economic youth the positive, academically focused peer groups that many of their wealthy suburban counterparts take for granted. These types of cohorts can push the students to excel academically (and provide academic role models) without making them feel ostracized for being different. This is essentially what happened when these students made it to exclusive high school or college environments, or when they participated in academically focused clubs and organizations. This goal can be effectuated by creating more organizations that bring together academically talented youth, and place them in positions were excelling academically is a shared goal.

Recruiting these types of students may mean providing them with incentives (scholarships, access to technology, exposure to elite institutions, etc.) that would make joining the group desirable, and provide a sense of exclusivity. Regardless of how it is done, engineering the collective muscle of group momentum toward academic goals would prove powerful in the process of encouraging resilience on a greater scale because the students would be able to be both academically talented and part of the "in" crowd.

Minimize Financial Stress: While the students were often initially reluctant to discuss it, anger and resentment over lack of funds and access to goods deemed important to their success was apparent. A large percentage of these students (96%) identified lack of money (and access to resources) as a major impediment to their school success. Given that one of the study pre-requisites was coming from a low socioeconomic background, issues emanating from students' poor economic situations were quite common. Most of these pecuniary obstacles manifested themselves in students' concerns about being poor during their early adolescence and not having access to educational tools that they felt would have helped them compete academically. For example, thirty five of the students (70%) complained about not having their own computers, thirty (60%) expressed resentment over not being able to attend SAT courses or get private tutors (as some of their peers did), and twenty six (52%) longed to go to "better" private k-12 schools and/or colleges. Additionally, a good number of the students, 39 (78%) worked part time, and of those 27 (69%), reported that the time and energy expended working negatively impacted their educational progress.

Given the inordinate stressors and obstacles that these students must face in order to be academically successful, initiatives designed to facilitate their success should take steps to limit the amount of financial pressure and deprivation added to these students' plates. Particular areas to address are scholarships so that students could choose their schools based on fit rather than price, access to updated computer and internet technology, and modest stipends to keep students from having to work long hours while in school. While these financial recourses could not erase all of the risk factors these students must overcome, they would help level the playing field and allow these students many of the same benefits that their wealthier peers may take for granted, namely the ability to maximize the amount of time and energy focused on their academic pursuits.

A Caveat about Application

As with all research, the conclusions here are only reflections of the students studied and not necessarily accurate for all students everywhere. Additionally, because the goal here was to glean *shared* experiences of all fifty students in the study, the individual differences and nuanced reactions to risk can sometimes be lost. This having been said, the above conclusions should be viewed as starting points and guidelines, rather than absolutes. Any resilience minded initiatives can and should use the above conclusions, bust should also recognize and respond to the specific realities of their given context and objectives.

CONCLUSION: RESILIENCE PROSPECTS

At the core of the resilience movement is the collective ideological transition from our current state of being primarily deficit focused to evolving to the point of truly emphasizing potential. This simple but difficult change in focus would allow us to really see the possibility in all of our students, and then act with that possibility at the forefront of our minds. While this is an invaluable mental shift, what we must guard against is dismissing or trivializing the depth, virility, and ubiquity of the obstacles that the students must endure. To tell a potentially resilient student who just lost his older brother to a meaningless gang war to simply "focus on the positive" is as demeaning as it is ineffective. As a result, in order for future resilience endeavors to be successful, a delicate balance between focusing on potential and recognizing the reality of risk must be established. The ability to strategically and effectively manage this balancing act is among the most difficult requirements of resilience facilitation.

Despite the inherent challenge to taking on resilience efforts, or perhaps because of them, there does exist enormous power to dramatically change the lives of students who are precariously positioned at various types of crossroads in their lives. The difference between spending the year after high school hanging out at the park in between basketball games, as compared to hanging out in the student union in between classes, can be enormous. And often, as we have seen with the students in this study, where these students do end up hanging out can be determined by a few caring educators, a program that is funded another year, and/or the cultivation of a truly positive self-esteem.

The notion that promoting resilience is essentially that of "saving lives" is a bit melodramatic, but at times (both literally and figuratively) this may very well be the case.

Appendix A

Resilient Students'
Demographic Information

Appendix A. Ethnic Background*/Parental Status/Parents' Education Level (N = 50)

Ethnic/Racial Background (Self-Identified)	Female	Male	Two Parent Household	Single Parent (Mom)	Single Parent (Dad)	Highest Education Level	Parents Student Home Locale
21 African-American	12	9	7	14	0	72% HS 22% 8th gr 8% SC	16 U 4 S 1 R
20 Hispanic**	12	8	12	8	0	60% HS 29% 8th gr 11% SC	19 U 1 S
5 Bi-Racial***	4	1	3	2	0	60% HS 40% SC 1 R	1 U 3 S
2 Haitian-American	2	0	1	1	0	100% HS	2 U
1 Jamaican-American	0	1	0	1	0	100% SC	1 U
1 Guyanese-American	1	0	1	0	0	100% HS	1 U
Total	31	19	24	26	0		

*Ethnic background was determined by the students' self-identification

**7 Dominican-American, 9 Puerto Rican, 1 Ecuadorian-American, 1 Mexican-American, 1 Cuban-American

*** 4 White mother/Black father, 1 White father/Black mother

SC = Some college, HS = Completed, 8th gr. = Up to Grade 8, U = Urban, S = Suburban, R = Rural

Appendix B

The Resilience Cycle

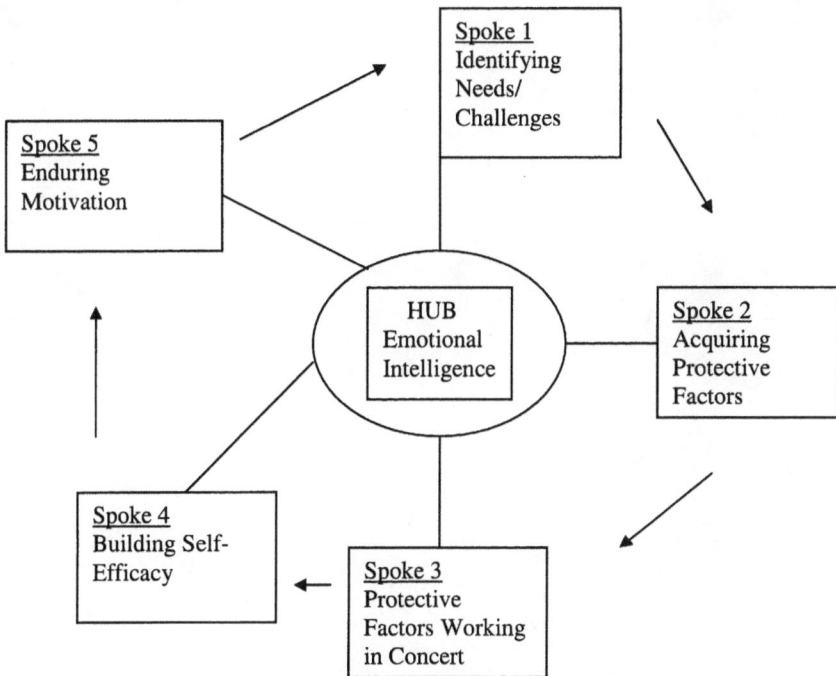

Spoke 1
Identifying
Needs/
Challenges

Spoke 5
Enduring
Motivation

HUB
Emotional
Intelligence

Spoke 2
Acquiring
Protective
Factors

Spoke 4
Building Self-
Efficacy

Spoke 3
Protective
Factors Working
in Concert

Appendix C

Resilient Students' Institutional Data

Appendix C. Student Sample N=50

Female	Male	Highly Selective Private University	Selective Private University	Public Community College	Selective Public University	Avg. GPA
31	19	5	21	8	16	3.356

Appendix D

Resilient Students and Major Protective Factors

Appendix D. N= 50/ Major Protective Factors = 23/"Major" = > 25% of Students Identified It as Essential to Their Academic Achievement

Major Protective Factors	Males (N= 19) *# and %*	Females (N=31) *# and %*	Total (N=50) *# and %*
Dispositional			
Desire/willingness to "class jump"	18 (94.7%)	29 (93.5%)	47 (94%)
Persistence	17 (89.4%)	30 (96.7%)	47 (94%)
Sense of obligation to one's family	17 (89.4%)	30 (96.7)	47 (94%)
High self-esteem	18 (94.7%)	28 (90.3%)	46 (92%)
Internal locus of control	17 (89.4%)	29 (93.5%)	46 (92%)
A strong work ethic	18 (94.7%)	27 (87%)	45 (90%)
Bicultural selves	16 (84.2%)	28 (90.3%)	44 (88%)
Strong future orientation	17 (89.4%)	26 (83.8%)	43 (86%)
Self-motivation	17 (89.4%)	26 (83.8%)	43 (86%)
Help seeking tendencies	16 (84.2%)	25 (80%)	41 (82%)
Development and explicit value of regimented study plans	16 (84.2%)	24 (77.4%)	40 (80%)
Affability	15 (78.9%)	24 (77.4%)	39 (78%)
High intelligence	16 (84.2%)	22 (70.9%)	38 (76%)
Sense of obligation to one's race/ethnicity	16 (84.2%)	18 (58%)	34 (68%)
Optimism	11 (57.8%)	21 (67.7%)	32 (64%)
Intellectual curiosity	7 (36.8%)	19 (61.2%)	26 (52%)
Strong racial/ethnic identity	10 (52.6%)	12 (38.7%)	22 (44%)
Extraversion	8 (42.1%)	12 (38.7%)	20 (40%)
Spirituality	6 (31.5%)	8 (25.8%)	14 (28%)

(continued)

Appendix D. (*continued*)

Major Protective Factors	Males (N= 19) # and %	Females (N=31) # and %	Total (N=50) # and %
Environmental			
Caring school personnel (k-12)	16 (84.2%)	29 (93.5%)	45 (90%)
State/Federally funded college bridge program and/or scholarships	15 (78.9%)	29 (93.5%)	44 (88%)
Attendance at a "non-neighborhood" school	14 (73.6%)	22 (70.9%)	36 (72%)
Caring school personnel (college)	14 (73.6%)	22 (70.9%)	36 (72%)
Tracking (High-level)	14 (73.6%)	21 (67.7%)	35 (70%)
Clubs/organizations (college)	13 (68.4%)	20 (64.5%)	33 (66%)
School sponsored tutoring services	12 (63.1%)	21 (67.7%)	33 (66%)
Attendance at racially diverse pre-college school	10 (52.6%)	14 (45.16%)	24 (48%)
Church sponsored initiatives	8 (52.1%)	12 (38.7%)	20 (40%)
Familial			
Parents' authoritative parenting style	14(%%)	27 (%%)	41(82%)
High parental expectations supported by words and actions	13 (68.4%)	27 (87%)	40 (80%)
Mother modeling strong work ethic	15 (78.9%)	22 (70.9%)	37 (74%)
Siblings as academic role models/trailblazers	9 (47.3%)	14 (45.1%)	23 (46%)
Influential grandmothers	7 (36.8%)	11 (35.4%)	19 (38%)

Appendix E

Major Psychological Stressors Associated with Academic Achievement

Appendix E. N=50
"Major" = > 50% of Students Identified It Stress Inducing

Major Psychological Stressors	Males (N= 19) # and %	Females (N=31) # and %	Total (N=50) # and %
Being a Spokesperson for the racial/ethnic group	18 (94.7%)	28 (90.3%)	46 (92%)
Sub-par pre-college preparation	17 (89.4%)	27 (87.1%)	44 (88%)
Accumulative stress	17 (89.4%)	25 (80.6%)	42 (84%)
Need to be bi-cultural	16 (84.2%)	24 (77.4%)	40 (80%)
Isolation in collegiate Environment	17 (89.4%)	24 (77.4%)	41 (82%)
Recognition of sub-par academic training	14 (73.6%)	24 (77.4%)	38 (76%)
Academic Competitiveness	16 (84.2%)	21 (67.7%)	37 (74%)
Cultural/Educational separation from family origins	10 (52.6%)	22 (70.9%)	32 (64%)
Feelings of low self-esteem	12 (63.1%)	15 (58.3%)	27 (54%)

Appendix F

Individual Student Demographics (N=50)

Appendix F. Pseudonyms/Ethnicity/Gender/Age

Pseudonym	Ethnicity	Gender	Age
Andrea	Hispanic	Female	19
Angel	Hispanic	Male	22
Antoine	African American	Male	23
Antoinette	Haitian American	Female	20
Antonio	Hispanic	Male	20
Charles	African American	Male	20
Crystal	African American	Female	22
Dante	African American	Male	19
Deborah	Bi-racial (AA/C)	Female	22
Denise	African American	Female	21
Derek	African American	Male	20
Diana	African American	Female	20
Irene	Hispanic	Female	18
Jamal	African American	Male	19
Jasmine	African American	Female	22
Jessica	Hispanic	Female	19
Jocelyn	Hispanic	Female	20
John	Hispanic	Male	18
Julie	Guyanese American	Female	23
Kerline	African American	Female	20
Kineesha	African American	Female	21
Lamar	African American	Male	20
Latisha	African American	Female	20
Lawrence	African American	Male	19
Louisa	Hispanic	Female	21
Lourdes	Hispanic	Female	21
Lucy	Hispanic	Female	19
Lupe	Hispanic	Female	19

(continued)

Appendix F.   (*continued*)

Pseudonym	Ethnicity	Gender	Age
Manuel	Hispanic	Male	22
Marcus	African American	Male	26
Marie	Haitian American	Female	20
Marina	Hispanic	Female	21
Mario	Hispanic	Male	23
Maya	Bi-racial (AA/C)	Female	21
Naomi	Hispanic	Female	22
Nancy	African American	Female	20
Natalie	African American	Female	23
Nestor	Hispanic	Male	21
Philipina	African American	Female	19
Richard	African American	Male	20
Ricardo	Hispanic	Male	20
Rosa	Hispanic	Female	21
Sandra	Bi-racial (AA/C)	Female	21
Santana	Hispanic	Male	22
Sean	African American	Male	19
Sharita	African American	Female	22
Stacy	Hispanic	Female	20
Tanya	Jamaican	Female	23
Tina	Bi-racial (AA/C)	Female	22
Wendy	Bi-racial (AA/C)	Female	22
N=50	**AA=21, H=20, B/R=5,**	**Male=19,**	
	Hat=2, Guy=1, Jam=1	**Female=31**	

References

American Council on Education. (2006, October). Students of color make dramatic gains in college enrollment but still trail whites in the rate at which they attend college. Retrieved March 12, 2007, from http://www.acenet.edu/AM/Template.cfm.

Anderson, J. (1988). Cognitive styles and multicultural populations. *Journal of Teacher Education, 39*(1), 2–9.

Bogdan, R. & Biklen, S. (1982). *Qualitative research for education: An introduction to theory and methods.* Boston: Allyn and Bacon.

Bourdieu, P. (1977). Cultural reproduction and social reproduction. In J. Karabel and A.H. Halsey (Eds), *Power and ideology in education.* (587–511). New York: Oxford University Press.

Coleman, J. (1990). *Foundations of social theory.* Cambridge, MA: Bellnap Press.

Conchas, G. (2006). The color of success: Race and high achieving urban youth. New York: Teachers College Press.

Crosnoe, R. & Elder, G. (2004). Family dynamics, supportive relationships, and educational resilience during adolescence. *Journal of Family Issues, 25*(5) 571–602.

Dubois, W.E.B.(1903). *The talented tenth,* Retrieved July 3, 2006 from www.TeachingAmericanHistory.org.

Ely, M. (1991). *Doing qualitative research: Circles within circles.* New York: The Falmer Press.

Ford, C. (1996). Resilience and psycho-social variables of African-American men. *Challenge: A Journal of Research on African American Men, 7*(3), 17–29.

Gale, G. (1996). Academically resilient rural junior high students: A qualitative study. (Doctoral Dissertation, Walden University, 1996). 9633566.

Gandara, P. (1995). *Over the ivy walls: The educational mobility of low-income Chicanos* Albany, NY: State University of New York Press.

Garmenzy, N. (1991). Resiliency and vulnerability to adverse developmental outcomes associated with poverty. *American Behavioral Scientist, 34* (4), 416–430.

Geertz, C. (1973). Thick description: Toward an interpretive theory of culture. In C. Geertz (Ed.) *The Interpretation of cultures* (pp. 3–30). New York: Basic Books.

Gibson, M. (1986). The school performance of immigrant minorities: A Comparative view. *Education and Urban Society, 29*(1), 262–275

Glaser, B. & Strauss, A. (1965). The Discovery of substantive theory: A Basic strategy underlying qualitative research. *American Behavioral Scientist, 8*(6), 5–12.

Goleman, D. (1995). *Emotional intelligence.* New York: Bantam Books.

Kirk, J. & Miller, M. (1986). *Reliability and validity in qualitative research.* Beverly Hills, CA: Sage.

Kitano, M.K. & Lewis, R. B. (2005). Resilience and coping: Implications for gifted children and youth at risk. *Roeper Review, 27(4),* 200–215.

Liddle, H. (1994). Contextualizing resiliency. In M. Wang and E. Gordan (Eds.), *Educational resilience in inner-city America: Challenges and prospects.* (167–177). Hillsdale, NJ: Lawrence Erlbaum.

Lincoln, Y. & Guba, E. (1985). *Naturalistic inquiry.* Beverly Hills, CA: Sage.

McCracken, G. 1988. *The long interview.* Newbury Park, CA: Sage.

McCubbin, L. (2001, August). *Challenges to the definition of resilience.* Paper presented at the meeting of the American Psychological Association, San Francisco, CA.

Morales, E.E. (2000). A contextual understanding of the process of educational resilience: High achieving Dominican American students and the resilience cycle. *Innovative Higher Education, 25*(1), 198–215.

Morales, E.E. (2008). Academic resilience in retrospect: Following up a decade later. *Journal of Hispanic Higher Education, 7*(3), 228–248.

Morales, E, & Trotman, F. (2004). *Promoting academic resilience in multicultural America: Factors affecting student success.* New York: Peter Lang.

Rubin, H. & Rubin, I. (1995). *Qualitative interviewing: The art of hearing data.* Thousand Oakes, CA: Sage Publications.

Rutter, M. (1979). Protective factors in children's responses to stress and disadvantage. In M. W. Kent & J. E. Rolf (Eds.), Primary preventon of psychopathology, Vol. 3: Social competence in children. Hanover, NH: University Press of New England.

Spradley, J. (1979). *The ethnographic interview.* New York: Holt, Reinhardt & Winston.

Suarez-Orozco, C., & Suarez-Orozco, M.(1995). *Transformations: Immigration, family life, and achievement motivation among Latino adolescents.* Stanford CA: Stanford University Press.

Taylor, R. & Wang, M.C. (2000*). Resilience across contexts: Family, work, culture, and community.* Mahwah, NJ: Erlbaum.

Villanueva, I. (1996). Changes in the educational life of Chicano families across three generations. *Education and Urban Society, 29,* 13–35. References

Werner, E. E., & Smith, R. S. (1982). Vulnerable but invincible: A longitudinal study of resilient children and youth. New York: McGraw-Hill.

Index

affability, 33–34, 42, 43, 47
African Americans, 8, 43
assimilation, 3–4, 5
Asian Americans, 8
at-risk students, 1, 16, 74
attitude achievement paradox, 28
authoritative parenting, 33, 37

bi-racial, 11, 54–55, 60–61
bridge programs, 33, 42–46, 48, 74

caring k–12 school personnel , 33, 63
Cuban, 10

desire to "class jump," 39
Dominicans, 8, 10, 80

Ecuadorians, 10
emotional intelligence, 19, 25, 32
EOP (Educational Opportunity Program), 44, 46, 52
ethnicity, 10, 48

future orientation, 27, 30, 33, 45, 65, 70, 73–74

Gender, 11, 48, 50, 53
Guyanese, 11

Haitian, 11, 47, 61
HEOP (Higher Education Opportunity Program), 44–47
higher education, 44–47
Hispanic students, 10, 12, 27, 71

internal locus of control, 5, 30, 33, 50, 61, 65, 70, 73, 74

Jamaican, 11

Mexicans (Americans), 7, 8, 10
metacognition, 25–26
motivation, 11, 24, 27, 39, 45, 52–56, 65, 67, 73
mother modeling strong work ethic , 33

Native Americans, 8
non-neighborhood/non-zoned school, 33, 57

parental expectations, 33, 37
persistence, 27, 30, 33, 45, 65, 70, 73–74
Puerto Ricans, 8, 10

race, 10–11, 40–21
resilience cycle, 16–17, 19, 29, 37, 57, 62
resilience, definition of, 1–2

scholarships(s), 22–23, 31, 35, 54,
 58–59, 72, 75–76
self-esteem, 33, 47, 50–51, 61–62,
 70–71, 73, 74, 77
sense of obligation to family, 30, 64–65

White(s), 7, 11–12, 20, 22–23, 33–35,
 41, 43, 46–47, 51
work ethic, 5, 33, 37, 50, 73

www.ingramcontent.com/pod-product-compliance
Lightning Source LLC
Chambersburg PA
CBHW030656270326
41929CB00007B/387